Strategy
Traps

Strategy Traps

And How to Avoid Them

Robert A. Stringer, Jr.
WITH
Joel L. Uchenick

Lexington Books

D.C. Heath and Company/Lexington, Massachusetts/Toronto

Library of Congress Cataloging-in-Publication Data

Stringer, Robert A.
Strategy traps and how to avoid them.

Bibliography: p.
1. Strategic planning. I. Uchenick, Joel. II. Title.
HD30.28.S76 1986   658.4'012   84-48444
ISBN 0-669-09362-9 (alk. paper)

Published simultaneously in Canada
Printed in the United States of America
Casebound International Standard Book Number: 0-669-09362-9
Library of Congress Catalog Card Number: 84-48444

The paper used in this publication meets the minimum requirements of
American National Standard for Information Sciences—Permanence of
Paper for Printed Library Materials, ANSI Z39.48-1984.

ISBN 0-669-09362-9

The last numbers on the right below indicate the number and date of
printing.
10 9 8 7 6 5 4 3 2 1
95 94 93 92 91 90 89 88 87 86

To Our Clients

Contents

Acknowledgments

Many people have contributed to our thoughts on strategy formulation and execution. We especially want to thank our colleagues at Harbridge House for allowing us to test our ideas with them and with their clients and for providing us with candid feedback. Ernest Glickman, Deborah Cornwall, Kevin Leary, and Peter Patch of Harbridge House have been particularly helpful in developing some of the major positions we have taken in this book, and we are grateful to them for their contributions.

We also wish to express our appreciation to Sandra Scarpa for her dedication and competence in managing the typing and production of the manuscript.

1
Introduction

This is a book about mistakes—the errors executives make in judgment and action and how these errors can be corrected and avoided. Although every enterprise and every management team is different, business leaders seem to make the same mistakes. We know this because year after year in our consulting practice, we found ourselves giving clients the same kinds of advice about their business strategies. We finally realized they were facing basically the same strategic dilemmas, making the same strategic errors, and discovering the same creative solutions.

We believe mistakes can teach us valuable lessons about how to formulate and implement strategy. Therefore, the primary objective of this book is to share these lessons and discuss some common-sense approaches to business leadership. We hope *Strategy Traps* will take some of the jargon, mystery, and hype out of the leadership process.

We oversimplify some issues and some solutions. Because we're consultants—not full-time members of the business teams we describe—we are never party to all of the facts. Therefore, we never know all the reasons for certain decision and certain actions; we can only guess. Nevertheless, both of us have seen—and have even participated in—most of the mistakes described in this book. The solutions we suggest—the ways to avoid the strategy traps—have been tested in the real world. We know that they work. They have worked for our clients, and we're confident they can work for others.

Because this book is based exclusively on our consulting experiences, there is no underlying conceptual model or framework that we are trying to fit or prove or push. There is no "grand scheme." However, we have had two fundamental insights about business strategy. The first is fairly obvious: Winning strategies have to be both well formulated and well executed. They have to be correct for the business, and they also have to be correct for the business team (the whole team, not just the big shots at the very top of the organization). If a strategy looks great on paper but can't or won't be well executed, it will probably fail. Likewise, no matter how well executed a misconceived strategy is, it will not win. Therefore, we've organized our strategy traps into formulation traps and implementation traps. Both elements of strategy must be done right to win in today's highly competitive environment.

The second insight may be less obvious (it was to us at first): The best way to build a winning strategy is to focus on avoiding the implementation traps. Not that they are somehow more important than the formulation traps—they aren't. However, *fixing* a strategy always comes down to the need for executional excellence, and by focusing on the barriers to good implementation, managers will be focusing on the strategy-building *process*. We have come to believe that such a process bias is appropriate—that it makes for winning strategies. The process of a strategy's formulation is often the single most important factor contributing to its success. By concentrating on process rather than content, senior executives automatically avoid some of the most pervasive formulation *and* implementation strategy traps.

The "Perfect" Process

What do we mean when we say that the *process* of building a winning strategy is more important than the actual *content* of the strategy? Is there a "perfect" strategy-building process? After studying dozens of management teams struggling to avoid (or get themselves out of) strategy traps, we have concluded that the most effective process has three components—important *intellectual, interpersonal,* and *leadership* processes that must be blended together to form an overall process for building a winning strategy.

We discuss the need for a rigorous intellectual process at length in Part I. Successful strategies are conceptually sound; that is, they make sense. Formulating winning strategies requires the discipline provided by a model or framework that forces senior executives to ask the right questions about the business. We've tried to capture the essense of this kind of intellectual process in our "Commonsense Approach" to formulating strategy and in our strategic planning model (see chapter 7).

Our experience is that, in addition to intellectual integrity, building successful strategies requires a certain kind of interpersonal process among the managers of the business. We don't have any particular model in mind, but we have tried to describe the interpersonal dos and don'ts throughout this book. At a minimum, the "perfect" process requires high levels of participation from all members of the business team; it should involve the use of strategic planning conferences so that ideas can be openly challenged; and it should emphasize implementation issues so that strategies are made more consistent with the talents and resources of the business team.

The final component of the "perfect" strategy-building process is the hardest to describe. We call it *leadership*. We have seen many business teams following an intellectually and interpersonally sound process but failing to build a winning strategy. In our opinion, the missing ingredient has been the driving energy, charisma, and commitment at the very top of the organization. Without this, strategies seem to fall flat. Companies that have created and executed winning strategies are distinguished by their strong leaders. Executives like PepsiCo's Wayne Calloway and Roger Enrico, Rockwell's Don Beall and Bob Anderson, and Citibank's Walter Wriston are role models. Somehow, they manage to convince entire organizations to follow them and make their companies' strategies work.

We don't offer any special prescription for companies that lack this kind of leadership process. They must recruit and promote executives who are more than individual contributors—who have the skills to get the entire team to function at its full potential and who can articulate a vision and convey a sense of mission. They need executives who have an innate sensitivity to the people side of the business and who appreciate the intangibles (see chapter 6).

There really is no "perfect" strategy-building process that will work for every business. However, we have tried to highlight the intellectual, interpersonal, and leadership aspects of strategy building so that managers can avoid the fifteen most common strategy traps.

Traps in Formulating Strategy

The strategy formulation traps are divided into two categories that reflect the two fundamental objectives of a business enterprise: growth and profitability. Chapter 2 describes three traps that deal with the challenges of growing the business. Trap #1, "Bigger Is Better," involves, among other things, the common assumption that costs decrease as the overall size of the business increases. Though sometimes accurate, this reasoning becomes a trap when some costs are sensitive to factors other than volume or market share. The management expense of operating a larger business, particularly one predicated on shared costs or on leveraging overhead costs, is frequently not factored into growth strategies. As a result, when the business grows larger, profit performance deteriorates. Understanding cost dynamics—how each cost component of the cost base responds to scale—and reconfiguring the cost base (if possible) are the best ways out of this strategy trap.

The second trap in formulating strategy is "Spreading Yourself Too Thin." This is another very common trap in enterprises pushing for rapid growth. This trap is more than a matter of simply growing too fast. It is triggered when businesses fail to analyze buyer groups, define the target market, and manage an efficient distribution system. In their efforts to serve the needs of too broad a market, many businesses fail to serve the needs of any. Thus, they become vulnerable to a focused strategy by their competitors. Unused computer capacity is put to work doing something unrelated to the core business; new products are added to the distribution system because executives think it doesn't cost them anything to add on; and so on. Such efforts usually dilute, then destroy, the validity of most strategies. They confuse the organization and erode the customer's perception of business coherence. Avoiding this trap requires that executives make difficult trade-offs, and these trade-offs depend on the use of a highly disciplined strategy formulation process.

The third strategy formulation trap for executives trying to build a business is called "Stuck in the Middle." This is the classic strategy trap that Michael Porter (1980) describes so well. It occurs when the business tries to be *both* a cost leader and a differentiator and, as a result, achieves neither goal. Investment and marketing policies are inconsistent, and competitive advantage is usually lost on both fronts. Costs are too high for the company to be a low-cost producer but not high enough to create a defendable position based on differentiation. As with the "spreading yourself too thin" trap, the way to avoid getting "stuck in the middle" is to make tough strategic decisions *before* significant resources have been committed.

The remaining four traps in formulating strategy, described in chapter 3, concern the challenge of increasing profitability rather than growth. Trap #4, "Not Being Customer-Driven," occurs when executives become too product-focused or "fall in love" with technology and start to miss what the customer is saying. They fail to understand customer needs and problems, and, as a result, fail to develop an offer that customers really value. Avoiding this trap requires more than detailed consumer research. It requires a kind of customer-sensitive leadership that is not found in many large, centralized corporations.

Strategy Trap #5, "Cheaper Is Better," is an especially important trap to avoid as businesses move into unfamiliar products and markets. To the extent that pricing decisions are based on costs, our experience is that businesses seldom understand their costs very well. Executives think in terms of accounting costs, not a value chain, and they have so many shared costs that allocations are suspect and product line profitability estimates become problematic. Strategic pricing is the best way to maximize competitive advantage. This means viewing pricing decisions in the broadest possible context, which in turn requires a careful analysis of business priorities.

Strategy Trap #6, "Underestimating the Competition," occurs when executive teams, especially those long associated with the business, make the assumption that their product offering is unique. A failure to understand the role of substitute products, the buyer's value chain, and the ever-increasing sophistication of competitors leaves such executive teams vulnerable and exposed. Higher profits are always projected for the next year but are never realized. Even highly successful organizations can underestimate a competitor's tenacity or willingness to take losses to protect or gain market share. Unemotional and systematic competitor analysis is the only way out of this strategy trap.

The final strategy formulation is called "If It Ain't Broke, Don't Fix It." Like the trap of "underestimating the competition," this trap prevents a company from capitalizing on profit opportunities because senior managers stop looking outward and lose touch with the reasons they are successful. When executives assume that because their business is healthy today, it will be healthy tomorrow, they become complacent. They start administering the business rather than managing it. Avoiding this trap is difficult, because the existing strategy *is* working. We recommend an annual strategic review of business opportunities as the best forum to discover what's "broke" and what needs to be "fixed."

Traps in Implementing Strategy

The eight traps we've seen managers fall into when trying to execute a business strategy are organized into three areas. The first area, described in chapter 4, involves failures in communicating the strategy. Chapter 5 describes the second area—failure in redefining the standards of performance. The third area, covered in chapter 6, involves the importance of managing the intangible aspects of the business.

Communicating Strategy

Strategy Trap #8, "What They Don't Know Won't Hurt Them," involves the common assumption that the only members of the organization who *really* have to understand the strategy are the senior managers. When other managers and employees are uninformed about the strategic priorities or long-term direction of the firm, executives often find that implementation of their strategy is clumsy and ineffective. It is usually costly to keep employees in the dark about strategy. Widespread communication of the strategy is the best mechanism for ensuring enthusiastic and creative execution.

Strategy Trap #9, "Sloppy Communication," also relates to the inability to communicate a clear sense of direction. No matter how brilliant the strategy may be, unless the business team understands and accepts it, performance will suffer. It sometimes seems that executives assume that their management team can read their minds. Communication of the strategy is incomplete and sloppy. Key words, phrases, or strategic concepts are ill defined, thus leaving lower level managers too much room for misunderstanding. The best way to avoid this strategy trap is to utilize a highly participative approach to strategy formulation and to stress direct, face-to-face communication processes.

Strategy Trap #10, "Eloquence is Everything," is the opposite of the other two common communication traps. Executives who fall into this trap are so excited about their business strategy that they fail to involve others in the formulation process. They and their top advisors believe they can sell the rest of the organization on the strategy by using elaborate and eloquent communications mechanisms *after* the strategy has been formulated. However, there is no substitute for participation in the strategy formulation process, and executives who fall into the "eloquence is everything" trap often leave members of the organization unmotivated, uncommitted, and frustrated.

Redefining Standards
Chapter 5 describes two traps involving the importance of establishing new standards of performance whenever new strategies are developed. Strategy Trap #11, "Failing to Raise the Bar," refers to the common failure of senior managers to upgrade their organizations—asking more of each employee—to match the demands of a new strategy. Higher standards must be communicated and enforced with vigor. "Failing to raise the bar" means settling for yesterday's definition of excellence, rather than tomorrow's.

The second issue in redefining performance standards involves Trap #12, "Making the Numbers." Meeting financial targets is always important in a high-performance company, but managers should never be forced to act against the best long-term interests of the business to generate short-term profits. Establishing a cost leadership position, for example, usually takes time. Market share has to be built, technology has to be upgraded, and so on. Reducing investment spending is usually the worst thing to do, yet this is often the first action taken when there is pressure for greater short-term profits.

Managing the Intangibles

The final group of implementation strategy traps involves managing the intangibles of the business. Strategy Trap #13, "A Good Athlete Can Run Any Business," refers to the common assumption that professional managers can transfer their skills to any business situation. Many excellent strategies fail to be well executed—or just plain fail—because of a lack of the right kind of leadership. Certain strategies require certain kinds of leadership. Differentiation strategies, for example, usually work best in the hands of a market-sensitive, creative executive. Cost leadership strategies require more discipline, more structure, and more patience. Paying attention to leadership styles and their impact on the culture and climate of the organization is the only way to avoid this trap. "Good athletes" can run more than one kind of business, but the best executed strategies (and the most successful businesses) *match* the talents, attitudes, and styles of the accountable managers.

One of the most difficult leadership challenges is deciding when to stop formulating strategy and begin executing it. Strategy Trap #14, "Analysis Paralysis," deals with this dilemma. Even the most action-oriented manager can be overwhelmed by great volumes of data. The explosion of information and its accessibility can lead general managers to rely too heavily on analysis. The result is a hesitancy on the part of the managers to take decisive actions—they are paralyzed. In many organizations, the need to create lengthy and detailed strategic plans further compounds the problem. In the end, senior executives must trust their instincts and sometimes must implement strategies without complete knowledge or backup data. This drive to implement sooner (rather than later) leads to increased experimentation and allows the company to place more frequent (if smaller) bets. Consistently avoiding the "analysis paralysis" strategy trap is one way to keep business organizations innovative.

The final implementation strategy trap is Trap #15, "Ignoring the Corporate Culture." Research and experience have taught us that most organizations have distinctive cultures and that strategies that place new or unusual demands on the values, beliefs, and norms of the organization will not be well executed. Ignoring these intangible factors is a common strategy trap, even though culture management has become a much discussed topic. Avoiding this trap involves making the corporate culture more measurable, more understandable, and more tangible.

How to Avoid Strategy Traps

Part III describes tools and techniques executives have used to avoid being caught in strategy traps. Chapter 7 outlines a strategic planning process that forces senior managers to ask tough questions about their business and guides their strategic thinking. This chapter is supplemented by three strategic planning workbooks (see Appendixes A, B, and C.) We have successfully field-tested all of these tools, and we know they will help executives formulate higher-quality strategies.

It should be noted that we have drawn heavily on the work of Professor Michael E. Porter (1980, 1985) of the Harvard Business School in putting together our strategy formulation workbooks. Porter's framework for analyzing industry structures and concepts of competitive advantage are simple, yet powerful strategic planning tools. We strongly recommend that executives familiarize themselves with these strategy models.

Chapters 8 and 9 describe ways to avoid the implementation strategy traps. Chapter 8 presents a systematic, step-by-step approach to managing corporate culture. This approach is based on 20 years of research and employs a tested survey-feedback methodology. Chapter 9 outlines twelve discrete techniques that can be used to deal with the turbulence and trauma that occurs when a new strategy is introduced. These techniques, based on the research of Dr. David Nadler (1977, 1979) and the Delta Consulting Group, provide a commonsense framework for managing strategic change.

Lessons Learned

There is nothing particularly magical or mysterious about the lessons to be learned from this book. Avoiding strategy traps requires more leadership and discipline than brilliance. We believe, however, that there are seven fundamental lessons to be learned about strategy traps and how to avoid them:

1. Most successful strategies are simple. They might start out very complicated, but they should end up simple and easy to understand. This makes them work better.

2. The keys to formulating good strategy are hard work, discipline, and knowledge of the business. There are few shortcuts or tricks. The deeper you dig into the basics of the business, the more likely you are to come up with a strategy that works.

3. Most successful strategies are formulated using group processes that ensure that the line (not the staff) "owns" the strategy. The days of elite staff groups formulating strategy are gone.

4. The strategies that work best are those that are almost over-communicated. That is, *everyone* knows where the company is going, what the priorities are, and why.

5. Executives must spend more time on the intangible aspects of their organizations. Half of the battle for strategic advantage depends on the quality of execution, not on the strategy itself. And executional excellence depends on such factors as leadership style and organizational culture, climate, and values. Understanding and managing these factors cannot be delegated to the personnel department. Senior managers must take charge of the intangibles with the same aggressiveness with which they take charge of the tangibles.

6. Organizational change should never be confused with strategic change. Many strategies require new organizations to make them work, but new organizations don't equal

new strategies. Without fresh insight and leadership, merely changing the players won't lead to a sustainable competitive advantage.

7. Successful businesses require strong and personal leadership. Being right is not enough. In our experience, there is no substitute for the vision, the dynamism, or the energy of the executive who can translate the "right" strategy into collaborative action. Rather than creating systems that deemphasize personal leadership, businesses would be wise to spend more time identifying leadership talent and building strategies around this leadership.

Part I
Traps in
Formulating Strategy

S trategy has received enormous attention in the past five years from business schools, the consulting industry, and journalists—particularly those whose itineraries have included recent trips to Japan. Books and magazine articles published during this period have made executives more *aware* of the importance of strategy, but few useful tools have been provided for actually helping them *formulate* it.

Our clients have found that most of the available theories, models, and guidelines either didn't work or were so divorced from the realities they faced that they weren't even tried. These experiences forced us to rethink the nature of the strategy formulation process and drove us to develop simpler, more practical models to address the difficult realities our clients confront.

We've reached four conclusions about formulating strategy:

1. Executive teams in a business usually have more than enough data to do effective strategy formulation. Any information that isn't in their heads is usually readily accessible.

2. The industry-specific and company-specific expertise of the executive team is the single most important ingredient in an effective strategy formulation process—and this factor is the one most often ignored by formula or "canned" approaches or solutions.

3. Effective strategies are best formulated by accountable line executives (with some help from the staff and outside consultants) and are "owned" by the line. Successful strategies require strong leadership, which requires early and active line involvement in the strategy formulation process.

4. The Commonsense Approach to strategy formulation outlined here has tremendous power potential. It borrows from existing models; it can be applied to a broad range of strategy problems; it is easy to learn and easy to use; and the results it achieves can be communicated clearly down the line.

The need for a simpler, more manageable, and less costly strategy formulation process was driven home to us by the experience of one of our clients, Rockwell International. Rockwell is one of the best strategically managed companies in the United States. The company has been actively involved in strategic planning for over ten years, but several years ago its executives discovered that the more they focused on strategic planning, the more complicated the process became. Plans began to grow in length. Operating divisions hired "planners" just to write the plans, and special headquarters staff were added to review them. Senior executives finally realized that they were not getting the required payoff from the process. The plans had become so cumbersome that line managers weren't *using* them to make decisions. Rockwell has since streamlined its strategic planning process, using its own version of our Commonsense Approach.

Our Commonsense Approach to formulating strategy views the process as consisting of four steps:

Step 1: Defining the business. This step involves describing the products, customer groups, and channels of distribution for the business. Such business definition details what the business stands for and what it is trying to accomplish.

Step 2: Identifying functional strategies. This step involves detailing how each function will contribute to realization of the business definition.

Step 3: Identifying sources of sustainable competitive advantage. This step forces managers to determine how the particular business definition and functional strategies will win in the marketplace. It also provides criteria for resource allocation decisions.

Step 4: Establishing monitoring and control mechanisms. This step permits executives to ensure that the business is under control and is meeting its targets.

During the past five years, we have worked with more than a dozen businesses in developing this approach. When the four steps are explicitly thought through and worked out, it can be said that the business has a clear strategy.

Our Commonsense Approach is admittedly simple in its elements, but it is difficult to put into practice. When it is used in conjunction with the strategic planning model described in chapter 7, the probabilities for successful strategy formulation are very high. The approach will not guarantee that you won't be caught in one or more of the strategy traps described in chapters 2 and 3, but it will let you know when you've been caught and will help you think your way clear.

2
Growing the Business

M ost executives want to grow their businesses. Managing a
larger business means greater monetary rewards, and more
important, it means greater self-esteem and power. Many strategic
errors result from giving in to this urge to grow without first thinking through the consequences of bigness and what it will cost. There
are conditions under which a bigger business will be a more profitable one, but there are also conditions under which this just isn't
so.

Strategy Trap #1: Bigger Is Better

In the first nine months of 1985, sixteen mergers—valued at over
$47 billion—were announced. Judging from these numbers, one
would think that most of America's business leaders believe that
bigger is better. Size is usually a critical strategic variable. Smallness
can yield strategic advantage to a business by allowing it to respond
quickly and flexibly to changing market conditions. Similarly, bigness often provides business with economies of scale. A significant
strategy trap involves the assumption that as the size of the business
changes, the same strategies will lead to high levels of performance.
The most common version of this trap is to think that bigger is
better—that growing big will provide you with clout or leverage or
power and that these factors, combined with the strengths of the
existing business, will lead to new levels of success. Unfortunately,
bigger isn't always better; the critical success factors for a small
business usually change as the business becomes midsized and invariably are different as the business becomes large.

A recent example illustrates this relationship between size and strategic advantage. A discount airline—we'll call it Angel Air—was established to service one region of the country, its target market being price-sensitive individuals traveling to and from the less busy airports in the country. In line with this strategy, its fleet consisted of only two types of jet aircraft and limited engine variety. This technology focus permitted the airline substantial cost advantages over its competitors, most of which had large, heterogeneous fleets. As Angel Air became more successful, it expanded its route structure and took on longer routes. This necessitated the acquisition of new equipment that could meet performance requirements different from those of its old equipment. In addition, the airline found that its reservations and ticketing operations had to deal with more complex routing; its crews needed training and cross-training on the new equipment; and the advertising vehicles for the new routes were not quite the same as those for the existing routes.

In spite of these necessary changes, Angel Air expanded. Its entire executive team seemed to be caught up in the glamor of running a "major airline." The CEO was perhaps the driving force behind this expansion, but nobody was willing to challenge the basic strategic assumptions he was making about the business. Because of Angel Air's rapid expansion, its cost advantage deteriorated, and it found itself in a new and tougher competitive environment. (Competition was much fiercer in protecting longer routes than shorter ones.)

The issue here is not the usual "growing pains" problem—investment and other costs of growth outpacing business's ability to sustain them. We are referring instead to a strategic shift. The competitive advantage the airline had when it was small (a lower cost base) was lost as it expanded, and it picked up no other competitive advantages to compensate for this loss.

In 90 percent of the cases, the "bigger is better" trap leads to unprofitable growth. Every once in a while, however, executive teams realize that size is not the only measure of success and we see this trap working the opposite way. Larger businesses sometimes decide to downsize in the hope of achieving the competitive advantages of a smaller business. Costs, however, don't automatically vary with size. For example, the corporate banking division of the

Chemical Bank decided it no longer wanted to make loans to certain sectors of the economy. In a thoughtful way, it proceeded to cut headcount (through attrition and redeployment) in its selling and collections departments. After three years, this division of the bank was no longer doing business with the undesired sectors of the economy, and all of the direct expense associated with those sectors had been removed from the expense base. Yet the division's overall performance improved only marginally. Upon closer examination, the bank found that its indirect expense base (e.g., MIS, financial control, personnel) had not been reduced to reflect the lower volumes of the division's new business definition. As a result, although the unit was now smaller, more focused, and even more customer-driven, its expense base was higher than that of similarly sized and structured competitors. It had not achieved the competitive advantage management had hoped for. Chemical Bank has now corrected the problem, and its corporate bank is one of the most successful in New York.

A division of Rexnord, Inc., stumbled into the "bigger is better" strategy trap in the early 1980s. Rexnord was trying to manage its portfolio of medium-technology businesses more aggressively and asked each of its operating divisions to maximize its potential. One division, which operated as a job shop had a reputation for manufacturing high-quality products and was able to market these products at a price premium.

Division management decided to greatly expand the business, capitalizing on its reputation for quality. The sales force discovered that it was relatively easy to bring in new business—although some price discounting was necessary. Unfortunately, division management found that operating a large job shop was significantly more complex and costly than operating a small one. In an effort to protect margins and control costs, quality was sacrificed. Soon, the division learned that the marketplace would no longer pay any kind of price premium for its products.

The division's executive team was thoroughly frustrated, as was Rexnord's senior management. At a strategy conference, they confronted the difficult choice of either downsizing the business (thereby allowing it to do high-margin customized work) or remaining large and lowering costs by introducing new process technology. In effect, the latter alternative would turn the division away from being a job shop. Rexnord decided against downsizing and invested in new technology, but the division has not yet regained its reputation in the marketplace for high quality and value.

These examples illustrate the failure of executives to ask what strategic advantage size should be yielding and how this advantage will change if the business expands or contracts. "Bigger is better" only when a larger size can be translated into a sustainable competitive advantage or increased profits. These advantages usually stem from economies of scale (in service, distribution, sales, or production), learning curve benefits, or increased opportunities to differentiate.

One final variation of this trap should be mentioned. Some businesses grow too big for their managers, and some don't grow big enough. Executives develop work habits that may be extremely effective in managing small or medium-sized business units, but these same habits may be quite inappropriate for running a large enterprise. Seldom do executives adequately consider the *match* between size and leadership style as a strategic variable. They should, for this match often determines the quality of the *execution* of a strategy and, therefore, its ultimate success. (This point is discussed further in chapter 6.) Sometimes, CEOs who are used to working through many layers of management and having extensive staff support lose their effectiveness in smaller, leaner organizations. For example, executives who leave large computer companies, such as DEC, to run small, start-up ventures often run into this problem.

The "bigger is better" trap can best be avoided by understanding the present strategy—why it works or doesn't work—and managing aggressively to obtain the strategic advantage that size should be yielding. Our Commonsense Approach to formulating strategy (especially Steps 2 and 3) should be helpful here. Before major growth strategies are executed, senior executives should work through how they will affect the sources of competitive advantage. In most cases, hard trade-offs will have to be made.

Avoiding the "bigger is better" trap is also a matter of managing executive ego. Because increased size signifies increased power and status to many executives, it is often difficult to convince a senior management team that they are falling into a strategy trap. For this reason, our Commonsense Approach should be used in conjunction with a broad-based, disciplined strategic planning process. We describe such a process in chapter 7. It provides numerous checks and balances to force management teams to examine the real benefits of growing bigger.

Strategy Trap #2:   Spreading Yourself Too Thin

The second strategy trap involves trying to pursue so many opportunities that the organization gets spread too thin and fails to take full advantage of *any* of the opportunities. We have found that executives fall into this trap for a variety of reasons:

1. They fail to understand the real strength of their organization, assuming that resources and talent can be directly transferred to new opportunities without loss of impact or competitive advantage.

2. They are preoccupied with growth and thus focus on the opportunities their business is *not* pursuing, rather than on managing the present enterprise. Even as the new opportunity succeeds, the base business deteriorates.

3. They believe that incremental business will leverage fixed costs and thereby lower the business's overall cost position. Although this frequently does happen, it is often the case that the cost base is more sensitive to regional share or account penetration than to absolute size.

4. They underestimate the differences in managing new opportunities versus the base business.

There are really only so many ways a business can grow. Whether growth is measured by revenues, assets, or number of employees or plants, businesses grow by doing three things: targeting new customer groups, adding new products, or increasing the number or types of manufacturing and/or distribution mechanisms.

These three dimensions comprise what we call the *definition* of the business. When businesses grow, they alter their business definition (sometimes without realizing it). Changing the business definition in any of the three ways will yield growth, but different definitions place different strategic demands on the organization. Therefore, it is critically important to know which of these dimensions is the intended source of growth and how expanding that dimension will affect the overall business definition.

For example, in the mid-1970s, Cramer Electronics, a distributor of basic electronic components, decided to add high-tech components to its product line. It found that the customers to which it was now trying to sell were no longer nontechnically oriented purchasing officers of corporations but engineers in the design and manufacturing departments. Cramer's nontechnically trained sales force was not up to the task of selling complex, high-tech components to technically trained customers who cared as much about performance as price. What initially appeared to be a simple product line extension to leverage the effectiveness of a sales call turned out to be an embarrassing strategy trap: the product line extension was not consistent with the mode of distribution.

Cramer management actively wrestled with the strategy trap they were in: selling a very broad array of products to multiple customer groups was resulting in a business proposition that was unfocused and that provided no competitive advantage. Fixing the problem would have meant downsizing the company, either by giving up certain customer groups or by narrowing the product line. Cramer was unwilling to do this. Management could not be convinced that giving up business would improve profitability. It is not surprising that a few years later, Cramer was in Chapter 11.

Thus, a good deal of thought should be given to decisions to change one dimension of the business definition. Substantial risks are involved in any such move—some of them potentially quite costly. Our experience has shown that it is particularly important that businesses considering such a move:

1. Make sure that the other two dimensions are still consistent with the expanded concept.

2. Make sure that customer buying dynamics for new products are similar to the buying dynamics of base customers.

3. If changing or expanding distribution, make sure that the incremental distribution is consistent with the product/market strategy.

4. If changing or expanding manufacturing capacity, make sure that any new technology can be integrated with the product/market strategy.

All growth-oriented organizations are occasionally caught in this trap, but there are a number of ways to avoid "spreading yourself too thin." In formulating the expansion strategy, carefully check the business definition and implementation policies to ensure that the expansion is as consistent as possible. Inconsistencies should be identified and anticipated before the strategy is executed. In many cases, the expansion strategy need not be changed, but the implementation plans should.

For example, when the consulting firm, Harbridge House, decided to get into the personal computer training business, we treated it as an extension of our technical training capabilities. Several of our consultants made it part of their normal consulting practice. It wasn't until we landed a major contract with the Sears Business Systems group that we realized we were spreading ourselves too thin. We didn't change our commitment to personal computer training, but we reorganized so that such training was developed and delivered through a specialized division. This increased our management focus on the business and helped us improve our bottom-line performance.

During the strategy formulation process, executives should listen carefully to their colleagues for any confusion about who the customer is, where the business is heading, whether volume or margin will be rewarded, and so on. These basic questions have to be answered if the strategy is to be a winning one. Sometimes, there are misunderstandings about these matters because top executives are moving too fast for the rest of the organization. They are seizing obvious opportunities to grow but ignoring some of the consequences of rapid growth. They are forgetting who has to *implement* the growth strategy. Confusion about basic strategic priorities is often labeled a "communications problem" by impatient senior executives. Just as often, however, it is symptomatic of an organization about to spread itself too thin.

Measurement systems are important in avoiding this trap. In the early stages of an expansion, the tendency is to impute only marginal costs to the new effort. Initially, this may be reasonable—the business can get people to work the few extra hours, the quality and service of the base business might not suffer by stretching the organization, and so on. Eventually, however, the expansion, if it is to be successful, cannot be run as a marginal appendage to the base business. It will require its own dedicated resources, and it will have to carry fully loaded costs. These cost dynamics need to be worked out up front.

The true sign of being spread too thin is a deterioration of quality and service throughout the entire business. The trick is to spot this deterioration before the business loses its competitive advantage. In our experience, it's very hard for top managers to identify the cause of the problem. They look for "quick fix" solutions, blaming the organization, suppliers, people—everything but the strategy itself. Their frustration is typified by the complaint we hear most often: "The business seems out of control."

The best time to establish control systems is during the strategy formulation process. Executives should identify the strategic variables that are critical to success and should plan to measure and monitor them carefully. Such control and measurement systems will often involve customer surveys, quality measurements, dealer focus group results, and other hard-to-quantify variables—as well as the traditional accounting data. Although the nonquantifiable measurements are more difficult to manage, they are the best indicators of a faulty strategy. If they are used properly, such control systems can serve as an early warning system. Corrective action can be initiated before the impact hits the P&L.

In addition, it is important that managers fully understand the cost base and how each element in the base responds to growth. Global generalizations about economies of scale will not work. (A useful approach for analyzing the dynamics of the cost base can be found in Appendix C.)

Finally, we strongly recommend using consultants. The problem of being spread too thin (like the belief that bigger is better) is frequently ego-driven. This makes it difficult for executives in the organization to confront the fact that they might be heading in the wrong direction. Even if some do become aware of the trap, it is difficult for them to confront their colleagues and their boss when their egos are at stake. Outside consultants are well positioned to take on this role.

Strategy Trap #3:   Stuck in the Middle

Our Commonsense Approach to formulating strategy argues that for a business to win, it must have a sustainable competitive advantage. In this area we've drawn heavily on the work of Michael Porter (1980, 1985) who argues that there are only two sustainable competitive advantages: cost leadership and differentiation. If a business cannot achieve either advantage for the industry as a whole, it needs to achieve one for a segment, or niche, of the industry. This results in four generic strategies:

Competitive Advantage	Served Market	Generic Strategy
Cost	Industrywide	Cost leadership
Differentiation	Industrywide	Differentiation
Cost	Niche	Cost focus
Differentiation	Niche	Differentiation focus

A classic trap, well documented by Porter, is being "stuck in the middle." By this, Porter means attempting to achieve the benefits of two generic strategies at the same time. What invariably happens is that the business achieves neither strategy. This trap is easy to fall into because, although it is necessary to attain the benefits of *either* cost or differentiation as a competitive advantage, a business must do so while maintaining *proximity* on the dimension not chosen. For example, a cost leader will be able to "win" by charging a lower price only so long as its products are *close* to the quality standards set by competitors. If the cost leader lets quality slip too much, customers will ignore the lower price and buy the better value.

The same is true for a company that adopts a generic strategy of differentiation. Hertz is a good example. The "number one" car rental company builds its differentiation strategy around its size (geographic coverage) and its commitment to superior service. Hertz usually charges a price premium. But this price must be close to the prices charged by Budget Rent-a-Car, or too many customers will abandon Hertz in favor of the slightly cheaper Budget offer. Budget, in turn, must maintain service proximity to Hertz, even though its strategy may emphasize a lower price.

Defining just how close your product or service offer must be to those of your competitors is one of the hardest strategic decisions to make. In many cases, it requires managing a subtlety and raises two basic questions: How much cost leadership or differentiation is needed to attain and sustain the competitive advantage, and how much proximity is needed? The answers to these two questions often determine the overall success of a company's strategy.

Generally, questions of generic strategy and competitive advantage arise as resource allocation issues. When there is not enough money to do both, should the business invest in a new system to lower its cost base or in a training program for salesmen to increase differentiation at the point of customer contact? Questions also arise when senior management is forced to set priorities. One quick test to determine whether your organization is "stuck in the middle" is to see how often priorities change. (If the answer is "all the time," you're probably stuck.)

We have been consulting to a nationwide finance company, owned by a money-center bank, that in 1981 made the strategic decision to achieve cost leadership. It reasoned that it could reduce its costs below those of its competitors by narrowing the product line and emphasizing efficient sourcing and processing of loans. As part of this strategy, expensive computer hardware was installed in the company's system. To justify this expense, the finance company consolidated its branch network so that more volume could be processed per computer. Operation of these larger branches—or megabranches as they came to be called—required a high level of management skill. The company therefore invested heavily in management education.

In 1984, after the hardware and software were installed in all of the branches, the company was confronted with the final phase of its plan to become a low-cost producer—reducing the number of products it offered. At this point, executives came to realize that their overall offer to the marketplace would be one of limited product scope (albeit at the best price). Management started to question the viability of a limited product line, noting that several of its competitors had actually *broadened* their product offerings. After weeks of heated debate, the company decided to make only a *small* reduction (about 20 percent of the total reduction originally planned) in the number of products it offered. This, executives reasoned, would allow the company to be "more competitive."

It didn't work. Our client ended up with the worst of both worlds, not the best. The small reduction in product scope caused the finance company to lose customers who valued a broad product line and one-stop shopping. These customers went to the higher priced but differentiated competitors that had very broad product offerings. The company also ended up losing price-sensitive business to the overall cost leader (which did have the most limited product line), because it couldn't take full advantage of its new technology and reduce its costs. Our client was clearly "stuck in the middle."

Executing a generic strategy means managing a subtlety. Organizations seem unable to do this unless a large proportion of the executive team is involved in formulating the generic strategy and wrestling with the meaning of the term *proximity*. Even then, the "stuck in the middle" trap is difficult to avoid, because it requires so much discipline to choose—and stick with—a generic strategy. In rapidly changing industry environments, such choices have to be reviewed constantly. New competitors can emerge that undermine a company's competitive advantage (whether cost or differentiation). In many cases, the best you can do is manage out of the trap quickly and effectively. The following are some key ways to avoid or manage out of the trap:

1. Always choose a dominant generic strategy. If necessary, force a choice.

2. Once the generic strategy is chosen, carefully define what *proximity* means for the business. Decide how close your

costs need to be to those of the cost leader or how differentiated your product offer needs to be.

3. Use a disciplined strategy formulation process that encourages discussion, debate, and resolution of these key strategic
issues (see chapter 7).

4. Analyze lost business. If you are losing significant volumes of
business on the basis of price and also are losing large
amounts to a differentiated competitor, you are probably
"stuck in the middle" and should rethink your strategy.

5. Don't hesitate to make tough decisions in allocating resources
in accordance with the generic strategy. Don't try to make
everyone happy or be all things to all people.

6. Resources in businesses are allocated every day. Even if you
are out of the trap, there's a strong likelihood that you'll get
back in it. Thus, a system of constantly reviewing strategy—
such as the one we describe in chapter 7—is necessary.

Summary

This chapter has examined the strategy traps associated with unmanaged growth. Executive teams that misjudge the costs of
growth, overestimate their own span of control, and fail to make
tough strategic trade-offs are not serving their shareholders' interests. In a strategic sense, bigger is not always better, and it's very
easy to spread yourself too thin or get stuck in the middle. Many
small companies have always known this, but awareness of the
traps associated with growth is growing steadily, even among major
American growth companies. Corporations such as Kodak, Xerox,
Polaroid, DEC, Wang Laboratories, and Avon have all recognized
the danger of unmanaged growth and the need to become more
streamlined. We predict that this trend will accelerate as senior
managers of such companies finally begin to define success in terms
other than asset or revenue growth.

3
Improving Profitability

I n chapter 2, we dealt with traps that are likely to be encountered
when growth is the major business objective. This chapter deals
with traps that are most likely to befall executives who are striving
to increase profitability. Unlike the pursuit of growth, the pursuit
of increased profitability is rarely ego-driven. It has multiple
sources: increasing the return from existing assets, responding to
pressures from Wall Street, getting a larger bonus, or managing the
best division in a corporate portfolio of businesses. Regardless of
the source, however, there are three strategy traps to avoid.

Strategy Trap #4: Not Being Customer-Driven

Whether it is the retailer who merchandises what he wants to sell
but not necessarily what the customer wants to buy, or the banker
whose product incorporates features he thinks are important but
customers don't, there is a persistent, strong, and increasing tendency among executives to formulate strategies without sufficient
regard for customer preferences, price sensitivities, and buying dynamics. This trap is so pervasive and important that it is the primary focus of Tom Peters and Nancy Austin's (1985) best-selling
book, *A Passion for Excellence.*

"Not being customer-driven" stems from two sources: being too
product-focused or "falling in love" with a particular technology.
Product-focused organizations do not understand what Theodore
Levitt (1983), in *The Marketing Imagination,* calls the "augmented
product concept." They look at products more as "things" than as
"complex clusters of value satisfactions." They therefore miss op-

portunities to add to or augment their product offering in ways that increase buyer satisfaction. For example, when a soft drink bottler offers merchandising advice and training programs to employees of its large retail chain store outlets, it has augmented its product beyond what was required or expected by the buyer. This builds customer loyalty. Being customer-driven means *always* looking for ways to augment your product offering. Cost and price reductions must also be examined, but they should be secondary considerations to cost-effective customer-benefiting augmentations.

"Falling in love" with a particular technology often distracts a business from its customers' real needs. For example, because of the volume of sheet steel purchases made by U.S. auto manufacturers, some steel companies focused too greatly on technologies that reduced their production costs. They "fell in love" with systems and steel-making processes that were very efficient, but they ignored Detroit's ever-increasing need for other services (such as more flexible deliveries, price and payment conditions, reordering responsiveness). When executives become so wrapped up in the technology of their business that they lose sight of the *benefits* of the technology in the eyes of the customer, they are in a dangerous strategy trap.

Many of the retailers we work with fall into this trap. In the early 1980s, we found that many of them were upscaling their merchandise content. Although upscaling was then, and is now, a popular strategy in the retail world, we were surprised to find so many of our retail clients trying to do the same thing—each in different competitive and geographic environments and each targeting different customer groups. We discovered that the logic behind the upscaling decisions of all of our clients was quite similar. These merchants, who were themselves upscale-oriented, believed that profit opportunities in upscale merchandise were as great as or greater than any other. In effect, our mechants decided to carry merchandise they wanted to sell, not what their customers necessarily wanted to buy. It is not surprising that this upscale strategy did not work for most of our clients.

Being customer-driven means understanding not only your customers but also your own product and how that product is used by your customers. What do they *do* with it? What does it *mean* to them? What *functions* does it serve? What part of your customers' total needs does your product fulfill? We recently worked with the industrial paints division of a major chemical company to help improve the division's profitability. Our client's customers were, for the most part, oil companies. These customers purchased the paint from our client and then hired contractors to use it to paint their oil tanks. To an oil company, industrial paint was a commodity-like product that was bought on the basis of price. Research revealed that although the customers were price-sensitive when it came to buying *paint,* they were not so when it came to *painters.* The oil companies found it diversionary from their core business efforts to bargain with and manage these outside contractors—they just wanted the job "done right." In response to this new understanding of their customers, the chemical company redefined its business from industrial paint manufacturing and sales to painting of oil tanks. The chemical company hired painters and sold a "bundled" product to the oil companies—painting of oil tanks. The market for painting oil tanks was not highly price-sensitive, and the industrial paints division is now a more profitable business.

The parent chemical company was so impressed with the performance turnaround that they developed a corporate program called Solution Selling (referring to the requirement that all divisions position their offerings to solve customer problems). The paints division success did not come from the R&D lab. It came from the minds of the division's senior marketing managers, who interacted with and listened carefully to what their customers needed and the problems the customers were struggling with. They then developed an offer that addressed these needs and solved the problems. They were customer-driven.

What is needed to move a chemical company from a product focus—the paint business—to a customer focus—the oil tank painting business? We have found that avoiding the "not being customer driven" trap requires two things: research and leadership. Every business should have formal, systematic research programs aimed at understanding their customers. The needs of *potential* customers should also be studied. Thus, the research should not only focus on product, service, and quality—as much research currently does—but should extend to understanding the totality of customer needs and experiences with the product. Such research will provide the necessary database for organizations to be customer-driven.

It is also important for senior managers to demonstrate leadership. Being truly customer-driven often involves breaking down established ways of running the business. We suggest the following guidelines. First, decision making and P&L responsibility should be decentralized as far down the line as possible. Otherwise, large and powerful functional departments will pursue policies that they think are for the good of the business but that often ignore important customer needs.

Next, executives should recognize their own product or technology bias. Every business produces a product using some technology, so it is not unnatural for executives to have a product or technology bias. Overcoming this bias means, first, recognizing it for what it is.

Managers—even senior managers—must stay in touch with customers. Reading research reports helps, but there is no substitute for direct customer contact. Executives of an industrial paints division must see what oil companies do with paint, just as retailers must watch customers selecting clothes.

Along these lines, it is advisable to hire new talent regularly, particularly in the marketing and sales departments. New people tend to bring a fresh perspective and often challenge old ways of thinking about the business. We recommend that companies orient new marketing and sales professionals by having them answer for themselves such important questions as what the customer is really buying and why—not just what the company is selling.

Finally, market research though invaluable, should not be substituted for hands-on test-marketing. The ultimate test of whether a business is customer-driven is marketplace acceptance of its product offering at an acceptable profit. Market research departments tend to argue for larger research budgets and more time. Executives must be prepared, however, to get their products into market testing sooner rather than later. This often means testing before the market researchers have completed all of their recommended research.

Strategy Trap #5: Cheaper Is Better

Every business engages in pricing every day, either by changing price or by keeping it the same. Although pricing is a complex subject, the literature provides little strategic perspective. Most texts address pricing as a complex process of bidding, negotiating, and buying. Regardless of the complexity, however, executives have to make pricing decisions and express them in numbers, and there is not a lot of room for subtlety. Stripped bare, the pricing trap most executives fall into is believing that "cheaper is better." The fact is that many businesspeople don't understand how to price.

The "cheaper is better" trap involves four basic issues: (1) knowing what to price; (2) knowing why to price; (3) knowing how to discount; and (4) understanding the dynamics of cost-plus pricing.

Knowing What to Price

Not knowing what to price is the most common way to fall into the "cheaper is better" trap. Many executives simply don't understand what they are selling or what their customers are buying. Two strategic questions are often ignored when deciding what to price:

1. How do you charge for the service component of the product offering?

2. Do you price to maximize product or relationship profitability?

Pricing for Service
Some businesses, to be cheaper than competitors, tend to give service away. They think of their product offering in an overly narrow way. Like the chemical company that saw itself in the industrial paint business, they focus on the tangible aspects of the offering and tend to ignore the less tangible aspects. Customer service is often viewed as a "necessary evil" or a purely defensive component of the product offering. When this isn't true—when service is highly valued—such thinking becomes a strategy trap, and incremental profits are forfeited.

To avoid this trap, a policy we label *augmented product pricing* should be adopted. If customers value service and perceive it as separable from the product, firms should leverage its significance and price aggressively for all services provided. In some companies, it is relatively easy to organize for augmented product pricing, and this helps rationalize the overall pricing strategy. For example, the Burroughs Corporation has successfully repositioned its field engineering services from a cost to a profit center and started charging separately for field engineering after it recognized the high value its customers placed on these services. Xerox has also successfully made this shift in its pricing strategy.

Even when service is valued by customers, many of our clients have found pricing for service difficult because the competition isn't pricing for it. Therefore, the competition must be educated. By using indirect methods of communicating with competitors, they can be educated to change their pricing policies so that they, too, price for service. The key is to "send signals" to competitors while avoiding any direct price collusion. Some of the most common market signals that can be used for this purpose are prior announcement of the new pricing policy, announcements after the new pricing policy has been implemented, and public discussions with the trade and with other industry groups to explain the need for new industry pricing policies.

On the other side of the coin, a business will find it difficult to implement an augmented product pricing policy when service is not perceived as adding significant value and as being separable from the product. In this case, a business has four pricing options:

1. Bundle the service charge into the price of the product.

2. Offer service insurance, thus permitting customers to decide for themselves whether or not to pay for the service component of the offering.

3. Educate customers to value your service offer, thus allowing you to charge for it.

4. Don't provide the service yourself and don't price for it. Rely on independent contract service firms, and simply inform your customers of their existence.

Product versus Relationship Pricing

The question of product versus relationship pricing is harder to answer. Companies such as IBM, Citicorp, Du Pont, and Baxter-Travenol Laboratories are all struggling with this issue. Managers of multiproduct businesses must decide whether to price each product to maximize revenues and profits by product (product pricing) or whether to price the package of products and maximize revenues and profits per customer relationship (relationship pricing). For example, one distributor of electronic components might choose to give its largest customers quantity discounts based on the customers' total purchases of all components. This is relationship pricing. Another distributor might give discounts only for items purchased in large enough quantities, no matter who purchased them. This is product pricing.

Relationship pricing works best when the relationship between buyer and seller is complex, time-consuming and expensive to develop. However, it is vulnerable to competition that focuses on the most profitable product in the relationship, aggressively discounts it, and sells it as a "stand-alone" product. Product pricing works best when the product is complex and expensive to develop. Product pricing is vulnerable when the buying or selling process is a costly one. In such cases, one-stop shopping or relationship buying makes more sense.

There's no simple solution to this dilemma. In our experience, executives who try to cope with it often fail to distinguish the real issues involved. We've found the most helpful approach to identifying the issues and choosing between product or relationship pricing is to think through the answers to the following questions:

1. Is our strategy based on product differentiation or relationship differentiation? Although they are not mutually exclusive, the distinction is very important for purposes of pricing. A more pointed way to ask the same question is: If we had to trade off one source of competitive advantage to gain the other, which one would we sacrifice?

2. What do customers really want to buy—products or relationships?

3. If given the choice, how would customers want to buy—bundled or unbundled?

4. How do we want to sell—through product salespeople, who maximize product revenues, or through account officers, who maximize account or relationship revenues?

5. How do we want to price—bundled or unbundled? Which pricing policy is the easiest to implement, the easiest to manage, and the easiest to change?

These questions should be asked *in order*. (The answer to the first question is the most significant, for example, and so on down the line.) By following the logic provided by the answers, executives can think their way out of the strategy trap.

Knowing Why to Price

The second variation of the "cheaper is better" trap involves the basic issue of *why* to price. Pricing is interwoven with every aspect of a business and should be treated as a strategic variable. Table 3–1 illustrates the relationship of pricing strategy to a firm's strategic priorities and objectives.

Cheaper sometimes is better. Knowing why and when, however, is the key to strategic pricing. These questions can be answered by regularly reviewing the relationships outlined in table 3–1 and by making sure that your pricing policies are consistent with the rest of your business strategy.

Pepsi-Cola may have fallen into this version of the "cheaper is better" strategy trap when it introduced its new lemon-lime soft drink, Slice. Slice is formulated with 10 percent real fruit juice (a combination of juices including grape, lemon, lime, and pear) and therefore appeals to consumers who are concerned with health and nutrition. It also costs more to manufacture than other soft drinks. In spite of this—and despite the fact that health-conscious consumers are notoriously insensitive to price—Pepsi chose to price Slice at or sometimes below the price of Seven-Up and Sprite. These were the brands Pepsi viewed as Slice's competition.

Table 3–1
The Relationship of Pricing Strategy to Strategic Priorities

Strategic Priority	Pricing Strategy
Sourcing new customers	Promotional product pricing: special prices on a few products for the customer groups you are targeting
Deepening penetration of existing accounts	Volume discounts and relationship pricing: special prices for customers that increase their business with you
Gaining market share	Lower prices: attracting new customers and/or increasing usage by making the product more affordable
Keeping potential entrants out of the industry	Entry-deterring pricing: lowering prices so that potential entrants will no longer find entry attractive
Entering a new market	Market-entry pricing: reducing price to a level that will allow you to gain market share over established firms in a new market
Differentiated product	Value-driven price: pricing that is consistent with the quality of the offer in the eyes of the consumer

Pepsi's pricing strategy was based on two "cheaper is better" assumptions: first, they believed that a low price would increase market share faster than a high price; and second, they felt that increased market share was a key to success in introducing their new soft drink. Although we agree with the first notion, we question the second. Perhaps the key to Slice's long-term success will be its "healthfulness" not its "lemon-lime-ness." By underpricing its value as a healthful juice drink during its introduction, Pepsi may never be able to reposition the Slice brand. We believe that the healthful soft drink niche will ultimately be bigger than the lemon-lime soft drink niche and that Pepsi has missed an opportunity to establish itself in this segment with a premium product.

It should be noted that our friends at Pepsi-Cola strongly disagree with us on this matter. We'll have to wait and see who's right. So far, Slice has been a tremendous success, gaining over 3 percent of the soft drink market by the fall of 1985.

Knowing How to Discount

The price of a product or service communicates many things to the buyer. First, price conveys messages about the cost of the product and about its quality. Buyers who are seeking high levels of quality expect to pay a premium price, and a low price often communicates low quality. Price also communicates something about the customer or the type of person who makes the purchase. Companies that don't understand and manage the total message conveyed in a price risk falling into the "cheaper is better" trap. For example, a large midwestern department store for which we've been consulting found that its white goods (linens, towels, etc.) sold best in a very price-promotional environment. White goods are now discounted nearly every day of the year, whereas 20 years ago they would be on sale only 20 to 30 days per year. The management team of this department store was concerned about how consumers were reacting to seeing the price tags on white goods with markdowns day in and day out. Wouldn't this eventually erode the pricing credibility of all price tags throughout the store? Because of this concern, the store decided to change its white goods pricing policy and show only the discounted price on the tag, not the original price *and* the discounted price. It initiated a white goods repricing program supported by extensive advertising and increased training for the sales department. In spite of these efforts—and despite no change in actual price—sales fell dramatically. Customer interviews revealed that discounting on the price tag conveyed to the consumer a strong sense of value. Consumers perceived themselves as smart, value-conscious shoppers, and discounting supported this image. The department store soon reverted to its former pricing program, having learned that cheaper isn't always better and that price communicates much more than cost.

There are three ways to avoid this trap without learning about it the hard way:

1. Conduct research to find out how aware customers are of price differences and what meanings they attach to these differences. Focus-group research is the recommended approach, not expensive quantitative studies.

2. If this isn't practical, new pricing policies should be tested on a limited scale. The test must be large enough to provide valid data, but not so large that it will influence or contaminate your entire customer base.

3. The final alternative is to do what the department store tried to do—educate the customer by means of advertising and sales force training. However, don't assume that customers will learn quickly. This is an expensive and hard-to-execute alternative, and it should be used only as a last resort.

Cost-Plus Pricing

Cost-plus pricing is one of the easiest pricing traps to fall into and often results in diminished profits and missed opportunities. Managers are usually overloaded with cost data, and it seems natural to use such data to price. Cost-plus formulas provide an easy-to-apply, controllable, and predictable pricing method. They also allow for a simple conversion of results to a return on equity figure—an important measure of performance.

Relying on a cost-plus pricing formula is a trap for a number of reasons. First, managers seldom understand their costs very well. Most managers think in terms of accounting costs, but these are usually suspect numbers, particularly when the business shares costs with other cost and profit centers. Cost allocations among these centers are an unrealiable guide to true costs. Similarly, many managers who use cost-plus pricing use *average* cost, when *marginal* cost is the more relevant number. In most businesses for which we have consulted, good marginal cost data were not available.

Moreover, a cost-plus price is not necessarily related to strategic objectives. Pricing is a powerful tool for achieving objectives such as market share or volume growth. By definition, however, cost-plus pricing is unrelated to competitive conditions. Pricing can and should be used to differentiate a product or service from the offers of competitiors, but cost-plus pricing is internally focused, not competitively driven.

Finally, cost-plus pricing is not necessarily related to the true or total *value* consumers find in the product or service. Most businesses end up underpricing their offerings when they use cost-plus pricing formulas.

A consultant friend of ours proved this point to us in 1985. This consultant—let's call him Dave—used to work for a large consulting firm that billed him out at a rate of $1,000 per day. Dave decided to go into business on his own. Because he had none of the overhead of the large consulting firm, and because he was eager to secure many days of work, he decided to charge a rate of $500 per day for his services. He told us what happened:

> My $500 per day figure was a cost-plus formula, and it was a mistake. First, at $500 per day, my clients thought I was a "junior consultant," likely to deliver lower quality advice and service. They were used to paying *at least* $1000 per day and equated high day rates with quality. Second, I realized my costs had almost nothing to do with what my clients were buying. Why, therefore, should I base my pricing on my costs?

Dave doubled, then tripled his day rate and has all the business he can handle.

Although some businesses are required to price on a cost-plus basis (utilities or government contractors, for example), we recommend avoiding this approach whenever possible. The pricing decision must be related to the strategic priorities of the business. In this context, pricing can be market entry-driven, share-driven, and so forth, to form a framework within which specific prices should be developed. Price should be related not only to costs but also to competing offers and to value in use.

Many cost-plus pricers believe that "cheaper is better," and they devote a lot of energy to driving costs down just so they can reduce their prices. In fact, many cost-plus pricers could *raise* their prices, but they are reluctant to do so for fear of losing customers. We strongly recommend that this fear be selectively tested. If it is valid, a transitional repricing program may be necessary. In any event, businesses should move away from cost-plus pricing.

Summary

From our experience, the best ways to avoid the "cheaper is better" trap are the following:

1. *Be creative in charging for service.* This may mean educating customers and competitors, bundling the service charge into the product price, or offering service insurance. As a last resort, don't provide or price for service; rely, instead, on independent service firms.

2. *Address the real issues in product versus relationship pricing.* Relate your decision to either product or relationship differentiation, how and what customers want to buy, and how and what you want to sell.

3. *Manage the total message conveyed in the price.* Conduct focus-group research and limited market testing to understand the messages customers read into your price. Use advertising and sales force training to educate customers.

4. *Relate pricing to other strategic priorities.* Make sure pricing decisions support the strategic priorities of the business—for example, sourcing new customers, entering new markets, deterring potential entrants.

5. *Don't use cost-plus pricing if you don't have to.* This internally focused, formula approach should be avoided. Pricing should be related to strategic objectives, the competitive environment, and value in use as perceived by customers.

Strategy Trap #6:   Underestimating the Competition

For years, U.S. automakers have been criticized for underestimating the threat from Japanese car manufacturers. In the past decade, similar criticisms have been made against U.S. camera, stereo, semiconductor, and a host of other manufacturers. We think the criticism is justified, but the problem is not limited to underestimating Japanese competition. We have found that although most strategic plans contain a few "fast and easy" assumptions about competition, these assumptions tend to underestimate the commitment, ferocity, and ability of competitors to protect—and expand—their market positions. As a result, businesses move into products, markets, and industries they shouldn't be in, and they are inadequately prepared to sustain the expenditure levels required to meet a competitor's response.

This trap is by no means confined to poorly managed companies. Public examples reveal that some of America's top corporate performers have fallen into this trap. IBM's entry into the photocopier business did not calculate the effectiveness of Kodak's and Xerox's response. Procter & Gamble's decision to go head-to-head against General Foods' Maxwell House Coffee with their Folger's brand underestimated the speed and determination of General Foods in protecting its position. It would not be difficult to come up with other examples.

Many of the business managers at Citibank admit that they occasionally fall into this strategy trap. Because the bank is so innovative, so large, and so sophisticated in its technology, it sometimes ignores or underestimates the product offers of smaller, local competitors. Citibank correctly assumes that no local bank can match its technology, but it sometimes incorrectly assumes that advanced technology is the major buying criterion. Many Citibankers will state that when "you're as good as we are" (and they are good), arrogance can set in. One manifestation of this arrogance is underestimating the competition. In many of the domestic and international markets it serves, the bank has had to settle for a limited market share, in spite of its advanced technology and its desire to grow.

Most executives think that they understand the competition. Our experience is that they don't. The only way out of this trap is to conduct a thorough competitor analysis, and many management teams are too busy or too lazy to do this. Useful competitor analysis is as much art as science, and it need not involve extensive, time-consuming research. We recommend a three-step approach to conducting this analysis.

Step One: Gather Hard and Soft Data

Hard Data
Collecting hard data should be the first step in competitor analysis, and it is the most time-consuming step. Although not all data are always available, you should collect as much as possible, by year. Examples of hard data include:

Competitors' financial performance, by product line, geographic area, and customer group.

Cost structures of major competitors.

Technology base of major competitors.

Capacity for innovation of the most rapidly growing competitors.

Distribution systems of the largest competitors.

Soft Data
It is vital that a competitor analysis include soft data. Unless these data are collected, the tendency will be to assume that competitors' future behavior will be a straight-line projection of past behavior. This tendency to make straight-line projections of the past is a sure sign that you are in a strategy trap. Examples of soft data include:

The personalities, styles, and ambitions of competitors' leadership teams.

Analysis of the dynamics of customer loyalty to competitors.

Competitors' strategies, goals, and objectives.

Competitors' marketing strategies and "favorite tactics."

Systematic analysis of lost/won business versus competitors.

Chapter 3 of Michael Porter's (1980) *Competitive Strategy* provides a comprehensive approach for gathering competitor information. Also, our Appendix B presents a workbook we developed for conducting a very comprehensive competitor analysis.

Step Two: Develop and Test Hypotheses

On the basis of the collected data, develop hypotheses about competitors. How will they react to a price cut, increased distribution, more marketing expenditures, and so on? If possible, you should test these hypotheses on a few selected accounts or in a limited geographic area.

Step Three: Develop and Communicate an Overall Competitor Profile

On the basis of the data and the hypotheses you've developed, make an overall assessment of how each major competitor defines "winning." This profile should include a brief summary of their strategies, their ability to execute these strategies, and their likely responses to your strategy. It may be that there can be multiple "winners" in the same market, and your competitor profile should help you define who they might be. The essence of solid competitor analysis is an understanding of competitors' most likely future moves, particularly in response to your moves. Armed with this understanding, you can develop competitive strategies that are more defendable.

Once the competitor profile has been developed, it is important to communicate it to the managers who are accountable for executing your strategy. It doesn't help the organization to "win" when key players lack in-depth competitor information. Firing-line managers need to know what to watch for and how to interpret competitor moves.

Strategy Trap #7: "If It Ain't Broke, Don't Fix It"

Successful businesses sometimes allow their very success to become a strategy trap. They become strategically complacent—resting on their laurels—and fail to search proactively and systematically for ways to improve performance. Strategies become rigid, and senior managers seem to spend more and more of their time *defending* their priorities rather than discussing or rethinking them. They resist making strategic changes until they are forced to do so by poor bottom-line results. By then, it is often too late to regain the lost momentum. The classic response of executives trapped by success is, "If it ain't broke, don't fix it."

Companies that begin to take their success for granted often lose the very sources of competitive advantage that led to that success. Some observers believe that one of our own competitors, (let's call it ABC), fell victim to this in the early 1980s. ABC grew dramatically in the 1970s by providing its clients strategic advice based on a simple but powerful model of how costs relate to market share. (In this model, the "growth/share matrix," the assumption was that the experience curve operated so that the firm with the largest market share would have the lowest costs.) To sell this concept, ABC staffed its projects with extremely bright and insightful consultants. It established itself as the premiere "strategy boutique." Unfortunately, ABC failed to sustain this performance. It didn't modify its basic strategic planning model, despite a growing body of evidence that the experience curve couldn't be applied to many situations in many industries. From our perspective, it also seems that ABC, perhaps in response to increasing demand for its services, began using more and more junior consultants to deliver its services. Although bright enough, these junior consultants may have lacked the maturity and experience to command the fees ABC was used to charging. By the early 1980s, clients reported to us that they felt they were not getting the value they deserved. ABC's profits and growth suffered. Today, ABC has shaken off much of its complacency and is delivering a more flexible package of consulting services that are value-priced. Despite increased competition ABC is thriving.

There are at least four reasons why companies—even companies whose business is strategy—fall into the "if it ain't broke, don't fix it" strategy trap:

1. Strategic inertia can be a powerful force, particularly to faint-hearted executives. Strong arguments can be made for *avoiding* strategy changes. Formulating and implementing strategic change is difficult and risky, even when the need for change is compelling. Fundamental assumptions are brought

into question, and the "fix" or cure is seen as worse than the "disease."

2. Many executives don't see themselves or their businesses as *leaders*. They are used to regulated environments or to being dominated by one or two major competitors. They wait for the government or the industry leader to change, then change themselves. Even if they spot a competitive opportunity, they overestimate the industry leader's power and adopt a passive, "don't rock the boat" attitude.

3. Some executives become so internally focused and transaction-oriented that they lose their strategic insight. For example, they attend to such matters as a new performance appraisal system, hiring of new talent, or a lawsuit at the expense of a systematic search for ways to create strategic advantage.

4. For too many executives, meeting the current year's profit target is good enough. They, and their companies, "settle" for last year's definition of success (that's usually when the current year's targets were set), rather than defining success in terms of tomorrow's challenges.

One example of a successful company that has been caught in the "if it ain't broke, don't fix it" trap is Tektronix, Inc. Stressing product quality, this highly successful West Coast business used to make 65 percent of the world's oscilloscopes. In 1983, several Japanese companies entered the market with products priced significantly below those of Tektronix. Tektronix failed to respond (its bottom line wasn't yet affected). But once the Japanese had grabbed over 10 percent of the market, the threat was recognized. Tektronix changed its strategy and began paying more attention to manufacturing costs and product development efficiencies. By mid-1985, it had halted the erosion of market share.

Several of our clients are good examples of firms that have learned to avoid this strategy trap. Citibank tries never to take success for granted. For example, it spent enormous amounts of money building its consumer banking business in response to an identified strategic opportunity, even though the bank's bottom line suffered for many years. In the 1970s, only Citibank dispersed the senior credit officers in its corporate bank throughout the United States so that they could be closer to their customers. This was done despite the fact that the corporate bank was thriving and successful at the time. Other banks avoided such geographic relocation because it was so expensive, disruptive, and painful. Today, Citibank's credit processes, built on the knowledge and experience of its geographically decentralized credit officers, provide its corporate bank with a significant competitive advantage.

IBM is another company that works hard to avoid complacency. Even though it dominates most of the markets in which it participates, IBM is always looking for ways to improve its product/service offering (indeed, this might account for its dominant position). It keeps its strategies flexible, never getting locked into a competitive position it can't change. Executives at IBM don't hesitate to innovate, even though innovation often means giving up a current source of competitive advantage. IBM wants to grow, and it knows that, in the computer industry, growth requires rapid change. The company plans to increase annual revenues to $100 billion by 1990; and by 1994, it plans to nearly double them to at least $185 billion. The motto at IBM might be "If it ain't broke, break it."

We are not saying that business stategies *must* change every 6 or 12 or 18 months. If the strategies represent the firm's best thinking about how to survive and prosper in its competitive environment, they shouldn't be changed. The problem is that environments change so swiftly—strategies formulated in October can be outdated by the following June. For example, nobody anticipated how quickly telecommunications companies like Northern Telecom, Inc. (NTI), would respond to the deregulated environment for telephone systems and equipment in 1984. It took NTI only a year to become the leader in shipments of business telephone systems. In August 1985, AT&T's Information Systems group was forced to announce the largest personnel layoff in the company's history—24,000 jobs were eliminated in a much-publicized cost-cutting move. This kind of layoff obviously represents a significant shift in strategy for AT&T. The fact that the move was made so publicly and involved so many employees shows that AT&T was caught by surprise. But the radical shift in strategy was necessitated by the radical change in the phone company's environment.

Some would argue that "artificial" barriers (i.e., government regulations) caused the complacency, the "fat," and the rigidity at AT&T. But there are ways to manage success and avoid the "if it ain't broke, don't fix it" trap, even in highly regulated businesses. We recommend that companies conduct an annual strategic review of new business opportunities. This review should identify, document, and evaluate potential investments the firm is *not* currently making. Such a review can be part of a regular strategic planning process (such as the one described in chapter 7), or it can be a special event. The important thing is that the review "shake up and wake up" key executives. It should force them to recognize their short-term, transactional bias and get them thinking about ways to improve their already well-run operations.

To ensure that executives think more creatively about the strategic alternatives available to them, we have found that a brainstorming or "mind-stretching" exercise is useful. The exercise works best as part of a strategic planning or review conference. Teams of senior managers should be asked to think creatively about completing the following three sentences:

1. *What if* . . . ? (Complete the sentence with the most frightening competitive event you can think of.)

2. *I wish* . . . (Complete the sentence with a description of your favorite dream or fondest hope for the company.)

3. *Why not* . . . ? (Complete the sentence with the most "way out," creative new product or marketing idea you can think of.)

Significant strategic insights can be generated from discussions of these three topics.

Even if strategy brainstorming isn't formalized as part of the planning process, successful companies stay successful by systematically looking at the *causes* of their success and constantly striving to be better. Ed Hoffman, one of Citibank's most creative executives, summarized the point: "No performance level is ever good enough for Citibank." This attitude explains the bank's strategic flexibility and its reputation for innovation.

Summary

Whether the challenge is to grow the business or to increase its profitability, formulating winning strategies requires an in-depth knowledge of how the business works. Line managers possess this kind of knowledge; staff experts rarely do. Formulating winning strategies also requires intellectual discipline. Very basic questions must be asked, assumptions must be challenged, and great quantities of data must be digested. Unfortunately, line managers seldom have the time or patience for this part of the task; their action orientation gets in the way. That's why strategic planning staffs were created.

The best way to consistently avoid the traps in formulating strategy is to use a streamlined, "Commonsense Approach" to the process—one that *involves* line executives without *burdening* them; one that raises the right questions without becoming tedious; and one that generates excitement rather than paperwork. We have introduced such an approach in Part I. It will be described further in Part II and supplemented with specific tools and techniques in Part III.

Part II
Traps in Implementing Strategy

Many companies fail to achieve their objectives, not because their strategies have been poorly formulated but because they have been poorly executed. Whereas formulating strategy is "thinking a good game," executing strategy is "*playing* a good game." Success in business depends on *both*.

Top executives run into three basic problem areas when they attempt to implement even a well-formulated business strategy: first, the problem of communicating the strategy to the organization; second, the problem of establishing new standards of performance—standards that match the *new* strategic requirements, not the old ones; and finally, the problem of managing the intangibles. The third problem involves managing such ill-defined, nebulous, and hard-to-describe variables as culture, values, and style—the kinds of things most businesspeople would like to ignore.

The key to avoiding these problem areas is very often a hefty dose of old-fashioned leadership. Unlike the strategy traps described earlier, there are few models or prescribed disciplines to help the executive here. Excellence of execution depends on having a clear understanding of what the problem is and on having the skill and courage to step up to the problem once you've defined it. We have found the following leadership rules to be most useful:

1. Overcommunicate the strategy. Tell people what the new strategy is, and tell them why it's important. Don't ever as-

sume that the organization understands anything the first time it's explained.

2. Get people involved as early as possible in the strategy formulation process. Get everybody "thinking a good game," and (not surprisingly) you'll find that they'll play a much better game.

3. Demonstrate strong personal leadership. Executives who expect people in the organization to act differently must take the lead. They must articulate and explain new performance standards. They must set an example. They must understand, through experience, what's involved and the price that has to be paid if the company is going to strike out in new directions.

4. Expect a lot of hidden problems. Figure out a way to measure and manage the intangible factors in the organization. Expect the culture, the values, and the informal norms to lag behind the new strategy. Set up early-warning signals so that you can respond to uneven patterns of execution and possible resistance to change.

The "how to" suggestions found in Part III of this book will help executives avoid the implementation strategy traps outlined in Part II. It is not necessary to call in a consultant to implement business strategy, but it is necessary to have a consultant's objectivity when examining your implementation plans. By learning from the mistakes of others, and by using the techniques and tools developed by well-run companies, you can avoid implementation strategy traps.

4
Communicating the Strategy

The best definition of effective communication is "the creation of understanding." Many companies fail to achieve their intended objectives, not because their business strategies are poorly formulated but because they're poorly understood—the managers and employees who have to execute the strategy simply don't understand what it is. When Chemical Bank decided to enter the discount brokerage business, its senior managers developed a strategy that focused on high net worth individuals who would buy and sell a lot of securities. However, this strategy (with its commitment to a narrow target market) was not known by the people who were answering the telephones and signing up the new accounts. Given this breakdown in communicating the strategy, it was not surprising that the bank's customer list soon grew to include many people who were not supposed to be there.

Strategy Trap #8: What They Don't Know Won't Hurt Them

In the consumer goods industry, business strategies are often poorly communicated because executives are obsessed with the day-to-day execution of marketing and sales programs. This concern for short-term results leads them to ignore the importance of communicating longer-term objectives. When they are reminded of this failing, the response is typically something like the following: "If I told my people all of the details of our strategies and gave them any kind of 'big picture,' it would simply confuse them. What I want is execution!" We have heard this kind of statement dozens of times in our work with consumer goods companies. The assumption is that knowledge of where the business is going will somehow diminish employees' sense of urgency. Consumer goods executives believe that knowledge of long-term strategy will force employees to "take their eye off the ball"—and the ball in this case is day-to-day operations. The trap is that the opposite is usually the case. Purposefully keeping employees in the dark seldom motivates them. In fact, it often causes confusion, and it always causes anxiety and concern. The net result is poor performance.

Some executives unconsciously fall into the "what they don't know won't hurt them" trap. They simply assume that their subordinates understand what the basic strategy is and why it was formulated. Unfortunately, this assumption is usually incorrect, and the result can be disastrous. When Bill Mooney assumed responsibility for Chemical Bank's discount brokerage operations, he discovered the inconsistency between its formulated and implemented strategy. He helped the bank rethink its business proposition and opened the channels of communication between the top and the bottom of the organization. When executives realized that their actual customer list was growing further and further from their intended target market, they were able to take decisive action. Mooney was instrumental in Chemical's 1984 purchase of Brown and Company, a Boston-based discount broker that specialized in serving the high net worth/high volume market. From a 1983 loss, the discount brokerage business has been turned into a moneymaker for the bank.

The easiest way to avoid the "what they don't know won't hurt them" trap, whether it was fallen into intentionally or not, is to involve as many people as possible in the strategy formulation process. When managers actively participate in the up-front business analysis and planning, the need for detailed supplemental communications is dramatically reduced.

A second way to avoid the trap is to document the strategy formulation process by having a secretary keep detailed notes of each planning meeting. These notes can then be distributed to a wide range of managers in the organization. The notes don't have to be neat. Unedited working papers convey much more than "cleaned-up" copy, often taking the mystery (intended or unintended) out of the strategy.

A case in point: The president of a $100 million metal-working company that was a wholly owned subsidiary of a conglomerate was extremely frustrated because his management team claimed that they didn't understand the company's overall strategy. Although the strategy was formulated at an off-site conference attended by parent company executives (with only two other managers from the metal-working company present), the president felt he had carefully explained and reexplained every detail of the new strategy to his management team. He finally decided to distribute copies of all of his working notes and all of the work papers from the strategy conference. To his surprise, he found that these papers were the best communication tool he could use to explain the what and the why of the new strategy.

, If an executive has deliberately kept the details of the business strategy from lower-level managers and employees to avoid "confusing" them, the only way out of the trap is to stop this practice. We have no evidence that knowledge of longer-term strategies in any way reduces the sense of urgency or the sense of commitment to short-term results. On the contrary, our experience with the Pepsi-Cola Company, for example, is that employee motivation and commitment both increase—as does the energy to accomplish short-term goals—as people gain a greater understanding of the longer-term strategy. Pepsi has recently embarked on an aggressive campaign to communicate its business strategies to lower-level managers. Not only has this campaign improved commitment, it has clearly contributed to better bottom-line performance.

Strategy Trap #9: Sloppy Communicatior

A second common failure in communicating strategy is to use language that is so sloppy that people fail to understand what the message really is. Words or phrases that may have a clear meaning to the CEO or the executive team are easily misunderstood by others. Jargon (or "consultantese"), which is sometimes used in strategy statements to impress the reader, is a symptom of the "sloppy communication" trap and should be avoided at all costs.

Sometimes, the strategy itself is clear, but important aspects of the implementation plan are not. That's another form of this strategy trap. A classic example of using sloppy language happened at a professional services firm we are familiar with. The firm's 1984 strategic plan called for a number of changes in basic management systems, including the compensation and bonus system. Ever sensitive to the anxieties created by such changes, the president of the firm circulated a detailed memorandum explaining the new bonus system. He said that bonuses would be based on performance (this was not new), and he gave examples illustrating the bonus formula to be used (this was new). The examples included such references to performance as "120% of objective" or "overachieve objectives by 20%." Instead of clarifying the bonus system, the memo produced a great deal of confusion. Surprisingly, the problem was that people didn't understand what the term *objective* really meant in this context. Until 1984, *objective* had been a term used rather casually between bosses and subordinates. Now, all of a sudden, this word *objective* was going to be much more significant. Therefore, the process of setting objectives was going to be a very different process. It was unclear from the president's memo exactly how objectives would be set or whether or not there was going to be a new set of "bonus objectives." For several weeks, there was a great deal of confusion and uncertainty about the compensation system. The new corporate strategy, which this system was supposed to support, was also beginning to be questioned. Happily, the president and the management team cleared the matter up as soon as they realized the source of the confusion.

"Sloppy communication" can also mean not going far enough in communicating. We have known executives who have been very careful in articulating *what* the strategy is, and they have even communicated *why* it was created the way it was. But they have failed to communicate the *so what*—the specific and personal implications of the strategy. This failure means they have not created the understanding necessary to ensure quality execution of the strategy.

We recently attended a staff meeting of a group of senior managers from a high-technology company. The senior executive had developed a detailed strategic plan with the help of his planning department, and the staff meeting was called to communicate the plan to key functional executives. After several hours of presentations and increasingly detailed discussion, it became clear that many of the key executives were arguing against the strategy. It also became clear that they were arguing against it because they didn't understand how it was going to affect them. They wanted to know much more than the *what* and the *why*—they wanted to know the *so what*. After the meeting (which ended before all of the strategy issues could be fully resolved), we discovered that many of the executives felt resentful and alienated from their own company. As one of them remarked: "I want to sign up for this. But I also want to know exactly what I'm signing up for." "Sloppy communication" can be a very expensive trap for this company to fall into, because unless these executives are 100 percent "on board," they will be unable to provide the kind of leadership necessary to succeed in their highly competitive industry.

Use of sloppy language and sloppy communications is not always an accident. Executives sometimes fail to define certain aspects of the business strategy because they themselves have failed to make fundamental decisions or strategic trade-offs. The most dramatic example of this kind of sloppy communication involves the use of the term *low-cost producer*. There is a world of difference between a strategy that positions the firm to be *the* low-cost producer and one that states that the firm will be *a* low-cost producer. The former is a commitment to drive costs below all others in the marketplace; the latter is a less exact exhortation to reduce costs. Whenever we see the phrase "a low-cost producer" in a client's strategy statement, we challenge the client to clarify the meaning of the term and eliminate any misunderstanding. It's much harder to achieve strategic goals when you haven't really decided what those goals are. Flexibility is not a virtue when communicating a business strategy—decisiveness is.

There are two basic ways to avoid the "sloppy communication" trap. The first is to supplement all written communications of the strategy with face-to-face meetings or conferences so that managers and employees in the organization can ask questions and have the key words and phrases and terms explained to them. Such meetings, though time consuming, are one of the surest ways to avoid this trap. The second way out of the trap is to have lower-level department heads draft their own statements describing what the strategy means to them. When these statements are fed up the line, top executives will have a valuable reality test of their communications. This bottom-up feedback process will ensure that the strategy and its implications are clearly understood and accepted at lower levels.

Strategy Trap #10:   Eloquence Is Everything

If the first two communications strategy traps involve inadequate, incomplete, and imprecise communication, the "eloquence is everything" trap is the opposite. Some executives fail to create understanding and acceptance of a business strategy because they communicate an overly detailed and overly complete description of it. The founder and CEO of a prestigious management training company admits to occasionally falling into this strategy trap. He is so familiar with the operational details and requirements of his company's strategy and so enthusiastic about it that he's often unable to communicate that strategy effectively to his management team. They understand where he wants to take the company, but they're not sure that they want to go there. An insidious mechanism is at work here: the more time and eloquence he devotes to explaining and describing the company's strategy, the more people realize that (to use their own words) "he has all the answers." It's not that they don't intellectually understand the strategy—they do. But they don't *emotionally* "own it," and emotional ownership is necessary for an organization to *act* on its understanding.

The purpose of communicating business strategy effectively is to achieve companywide understanding, acceptance, and commitment. This requires intellectual understanding, but it also involves something else. Employees at this training company want to "own" their strategy. The firm is relatively small, and the employees want to feel part of charting its direction. Even employees of large organizations feel somewhat left out and demotivated when the executives "have all the answers." In our consulting practice, when we hear what we heard from managers at this training company, we know that what they're really saying is, "I wish I were able to provide some of the answers myself."

The "eloquence is everything" strategy trap is an easy one for dynamic, entrepreneurial executives to fall into. Their impatience and their intimate knowledge of the business causes them to take shortcuts. They formulate the strategy (and often the implementation plans) and *then* attempt to talk everyone else into seeing the world as they see it. They sincerely believe that the eloquence of their reasoning will substitute for a more time-consuming and messy participative strategy formulation process. Even when they are reminded of this strategy trap, such executives characteristically reply: "Okay, you're right. I need to bring more people into the process. I'll bring them up to date . . . tomorrow." Our experience is that by the time "tomorrow" arrives, any chance for genuine involvement and participation in creating the strategy has passed— and most managers in the organization know it! It's very hard to *fake* your way out of this trap.

Once middle managers realize that they have missed the opportunity to discuss and challenge the vision for the future, they very often "tune out." Intellectually, they understand where the company wants to go, but this intellectual understanding is no substitute for enthusiastic support. Middle management communication of the strategy to lower levels of the organization suffers, and the only people who become excited about implementing the strategy are those at the very top—those who thought it up. Unfortunately, they are the *least* important group to motivate. Effective strategy execution requires the commitment of all parts of the organization.

Two things can be done to avoid this trap, and there is a separate action to get out of it once caught. First, a highly participative strategy formulation process is the best way to "sell" the strategy. This eliminates the necessity for detailed and long-winded, if eloquent, communications. If a highly participative formulation process can't be employed, it is usually best to have someone other than the chief executive officer communicate the strategy to the rest of the management team. The CEO generally has too much invested to be an effective communicator, and there is a high likelihood that people won't openly debate the issues with the CEO. Workshops or strategy conferences designed to establish a dialogue and create understanding are usually the best ways to communicate a new business strategy to an organization. The CEO can participate, but other executives should take the lead in explaining and discussing and answering questions about the strategy. This reduces defensiveness and avoids a reliance on eloquence to create understanding.

Charismatic executives can—and should—be used to articulate

a new strategy. Often, their images, enthusiasm, and excitement are contagious and can generate high levels of motivation. But even when a charismatic leader is the primary vehicle for communicating the strategy, it is important to follow up with other executives in a conference format. Only in this way can the real questions and concerns of the organization be openly discussed and dealt with.

Once a company is caught in this trap, the best way out (short of reformulating the strategy) is to step back from any implementation plans that were communicated and try to generate excitement and commitment for a more bottom-up set of plans. These plans should focus on *short-term* implementation issues. By focusing on more immediate and substantive issues (rather than the longer-term strategy itself), managers feel that they are engaging in genuine problem solving—and they are! Thus, "phony participation" gives way to genuine participation, and the issue of who owns the overall strategy becomes much less sensitive. The sense of disenfranchisement tends to decrease. Top executives must realize, however, that they still have a selling job to do on the overall strategy. Once middle managers get involved in executing parts of this strategy, their understanding and acceptance of the big picture should follow more easily.

Summary

Communication of strategy is the vital link between thinking a good game and playing a good game—and winning requires both. A high-quality strategy that is poorly communicated will not be well executed. A flawed strategy that is perfectly communicated will be well executed, but it will not be successful. In either case, the probabilities of winning are low. The grid shown in figure 4–1 can help managers diagnose their chances of putting together a winning strategy and identify the source of strategic vulnerability.

When both the formulation and the communication processes are done well, the potential for success is high. When they are both done poorly, the potential for success is low. When senior executives are frustrated with the organization's performance—when expectations are unmet and there are constant and negative surprises and

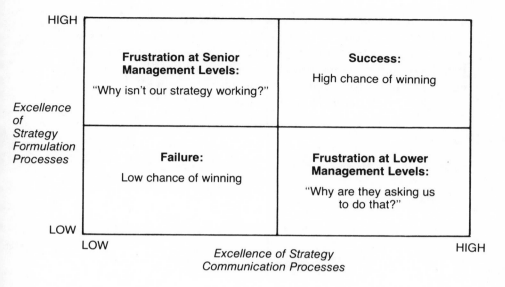

Figure 4–1. *Strategic Vulnerability Grid*

shortfalls—it is likely that the strategy *communication* process is at fault. Top managers know what the business should be doing. They've formulated a winning strategy, but the lower levels aren't executing it. Executives are left asking the question: "Why isn't our strategy working?" If the basic capabilities (skills, resources, etc.) are present in the organization, senior management has stumbled into at least one of the three strategy communication traps.

If, on the other hand, the business is less than successful, and middle and lower-level managers are the most frustrated—while senior managers seem to be taking performance shortfalls more or less in stride (often blaming "the economy," "foreign competition," or "a shortage of management talent")—it is likely that the strategy *fomulation* process is at fault. Firing-line employees and managers know that the strategy isn't right. They find themselves trying to execute a poorly conceived marketing plan, attempting to sell a lower-quality product (to customers who value quality) or trying to sustain price premiums (to customers who are extremely price-sensitive). In such cases, managers have fallen into one or more of the six strategy formulation traps, and it makes little sense to develop better communications processes. What is needed is a new strategy—one that is formulated more in accordance with the Common-sense Approach described in Part I.

5
Redefining Standards of Performance

Too often, executives who change their business's basic strategy fail to change the day-to-day standards of performance that support the strategy. A change in direction automatically means that different issues become important and that new priorities must be set. Factors that weren't important under the old plan (such as a new customer group, a product attribute, or a particular technology) may suddenly become critical to success. This shift requires that managers at all levels of the organization redefine day-to-day performance standards for their employees.

Executives fall into two basic traps in regard to redefining performance standards:

1. They fail to recognize the need for higher standards (or if they do recognize the need, they fail to act).

2. They recognize the need but redefine the new standards solely in financial terms. Once established, these financial targets become an obsession, and the organization loses sight of the basic reason why the strategy was formulated in the first place.

There are four fundamental "do's" for managers who are struggling with setting new standards of performance:

1. Always make sure that the person who is in charge of executing a strategy is thoroughly familiar with that strategy, believes in it, and has the skills and abilities to execute it. Don't

count on the team approach—implementing new strategies requires individual leadership.

2. Move quickly to replace executives who are going to fail. Don't make excuses for poor performance or try to "carry" managers who can't learn new skills. Move them aside if you must—put them in positions where their talents can be utilized—but see that they are not in a position to hinder the implementation of your strategy.

3. Always set qualitative as well as quantitative targets to ensure that all important aspects of the strategy are captured in somebody's MBOs.

4. Review the reward and recognition systems to make sure that managers are being paid to do what you want them to do. These systems usually lag behind the strategy by a year or more. Move quickly to change them so that the desired behavior is properly recognized.

Strategy Trap #11:   Failing to Raise the Bar

Every high jumper knows that there is a limit to the height he or she can jump. That limit is stretched by raising the bar after each successful effort, and sooner or later, athletes reach the peak of their performance. So do management teams. Unfortunately, as competitors "raise the bar" in business, some organizations fail to upgrade the quality of their "jumpers."

One of the saddest and most difficult consulting assignments for us is to work with an organization that has spent a great deal of time and effort formulating a new business strategy and then to watch that organization turn the execution of the strategy over to a management team that is incapable of executing it. Sometimes the team that is asked to implement a new strategy—and can't—is the existing management team.

We have seen this happen frequently in the financial services industry, which has undergone rapid and radical changes in the past five years. Led by innovators—such as Banc One Corporation, Security Pacific National Bank, and Citicorp—financial institutions have been quick to recognize the need to reexamine their business strategies and identify new target markets, new customer groups, new products and services, and new technologies. They have not been so quick to realize that these new strategies require new definitions of success and new standards of performance for key work units. Regional banks have been especially slow to move. Many have formulated new strategies, but few have executed them successfully. They are often led by people who attempt to get by without disrupting the status quo or who have ducked the issue of "raising the bar."

The Bank of New England recently fell into this strategy trap. In 1984, the bank spent a lot of time and effort reformulating its basic strategy. The bank was long known as a "bank of business," but the new strategy stressed nontraditional lines of business. For example, retail banking was to be stressed. By January 1985, little had been done to implement the strategy. Peter McCormick, the bank's president, was openly frustrated. He properly diagnosed the problem as an unwillingness to throw off the old order and adopt the new. What he failed to realize, however, was that asking the organization to move to a new order involved raising the standards of performance significantly, especially those in retail banking. In addition, almost all of the bank's reward systems and formal and informal performance standards were geared to wholesale and commercial banking. There were no retail banking "heroes," and McCormick's management team was not acting to create any.

McCormick and his top management team had tried to implement the new strategy without modifying the basic performance standards and performance expectations that governed the behavior of responsible executives. They tried to run the *new* bank with the *old* managers, who were both unwilling and unable to execute the new business strategy. Failure to implement the strategy was blamed on the pending merger with the Connecticut Bank and Trust Company (CBT). Executives tended to say, "When the CBT acquisition is completed, *then* we'll change things around here. . . ." We believe that was really an excuse for not making tough decisions. It wasn't until the issue of new performance standards was made painfully explicit during a series of strategy conferences that the executives understood and accepted that they were in a strategy trap.

The Bank of New England is currently managing its way out of this trap and has been reorganized to make it easier for key executives to accept new standards of performance. The reorganization included the eventual merger of the bank with CBT and the appointment of Walter Connolly (CBT's chief executive) as chairman. These events allowed the Bank of New England to bring in "new blood" and to redefine some of the rules of the game.

Another example of this strategy trap was experienced by Rexnord, Inc., a Milwaukee-based conglomerate. Rexnord spent almost two years redefining and redeploying its assets to lessen its dependence on the slow-growing heavy industries that had long been its main source of revenues. At first, Rexnord attempted to implement its new strategy without "raising the bar." None of its key executives were replaced. Robert Krikorian and Donald Taylor (the chairman and president respectively) continued to let the heads of business units set their own goals. They assumed that the new strategy would sink in and would motivate midlevel managers to behave differently—but this did not happen. Disappointing peformance in 1982 and 1983 was followed by the realization that some housecleaning was needed at the very top. Starting in 1984, more than a dozen key executives were reassigned or replaced. The message was quite clear—the bar had been raised and new definitions of success were established. But in Rexnord's case, it took two years.

"Raising the bar" doesn't always require a reorganization or executive firing squad, although these are the most common and most effective ways out of the strategy trap. The Pepsi-Cola organization has extremely high standards of performance and is somehow always able to "raise the bar" a little higher when it must. In studying Pepsi and other high-standards companies, we've identified at least seven other ways to raise performance standards.

1. *Use old-fashioned salesmanship*. Sometimes, executives can "raise the bar" and successfully increase performance expectations by effectively selling the need for higher performance standards. By creating a vision of the future, and creating excitement, executives can sometimes successfully encourage subordinates to strive for higher levels of performance. Asking people to "give it the old college try" seems to work in some corporations.

2. *Pay for performance*. Another effective means of "raising the bar" is to pay large, unusually generous bonuses for higher levels of performance. Executives can create "heroes" in the organization by promptly rewarding those who perform at higher levels. Singling out and making positive examples of those who successfully complete new or more difficult tasks is one way of motivating others to perform at the desired level.

3. *Scare people*. Often, people can be motivated to produce more when they are threatened. When the negative consequences of failure are emphasized, people often find reservoirs of energy and renewed commitment to higher levels of performance. If such scare tactics are also combined with and appeal to people's loyalty to the organization, higher levels of performance may be sustained over long periods of time. John Reem, president of Citicorp Savings of Illinois, used this technique effectively in 1985 when he sought to have his organization adopt a new marketing strategy. He made it very clear to all of his key managers that if his savings and loan organization did not decrease its operating expenditures and bring innovative new products to market, its competitive position in the marketplace would rapidly be eroded. This would mean that many managers would lose their jobs. He painted a vivid and bleak picture of the future without some "belt-tightening," and he successfully got his organization to adopt new and higher performance standards.

4. *Find a role model*. One way of convincing people in the organization that they can produce at higher levels is to isolate and identify a positive role model. With such a role model, others in the organization gain confidence that they, too, can perform. Often, hiring an effective manager from a competitor is the best way to establish such a role model. Once he or she is on board, let this manager set the new tone and the new standards, challenging people to perform at higher levels.

5. *Create an MBO task force*. Another technique we have seen used successfully is the creation of a task force to define new performance standards. The task force is usually led by a senior executive who appreciates the need for higher standards. But this exec-

utive does not arbitrarily dictate these standards; rather, he or she focuses the task force's attention on the *need* for higher standards and lets the members of the task force develop the specific objectives for the key managers of the business. Invariably, these goals are ambitious. This highly participative approach to goal setting motivates people not only to adopt the higher standards but to work energetically toward accomplishing them.

6. *Conduct special training programs.* Special training programs can be conducted to increase commitment and to communicate new performance standards to the organization. In an off-site training meeting, tough, clear signals can be sent to the managers in the organization about what is expected from them in connection with the new strategy. Besides communicating strategic and operating expectations, the training program allows for the development of critical skills. Rexnord, Inc., utilized this technique very successfully when it sought to implement new business strategies in its mechanical power and electronic components businesses. In conjunction with the training program, it was made very clear to managers in Rexnord how they would be expected to behave to execute the new strategies. Those people who were unwilling or unable to change were subtly encouraged to leave the organization.

7. *Create "penalty box" assignments.* It is often necessary to move executives aside when they are unwilling or unable to meet higher standards of performance. Such "penalty box" assignments temporarily remove people who stand in the way of implementing the new strategy and clear the way for high achievers who are more in tune with new strategic directions. Citicorp has often used this technique, and many of the most senior managers of that institution served for a year or two in "penalty box" assignments at one time or another in their careers. These assignments are often staff positions or less visible and less influential line positions. If a manager completes the assignment successfully, he or she is brought back into the mainstream and promoted (often without much "penalty" when it comes to pay).

If all else fails, the two most effective ways of shocking the organization into adopting higher standards of performance are to reorganize (thus moving out the deadwood and allowing the senior team to set new goals and new priorities and place new leaders into important positions) or to remove those managers and executives who can't or won't enthusiastically endorse the new strategic objectives.

Strategy Trap #12:   Making the Numbers

All executives must translate strategy into measurable goals and targets for their organizations. Such targets are generally expressed in terms of both short- and long-term "numbers." Once these numbers have been created, however, many business leaders fall into a trap of relentlessly pursuing them and forgetting about the underlying strategic reasons for them.

There are many classic examples of executives who have fallen into this trap. Back in the 1970s, we worked with a plant manager in one of our client companies who admitted that, on several occasions, he had initiated short-term layoffs of personnel in his plant to "make the numbers" at year-end. He had figured out that, according to the way labor costs were computed, such layoffs were the only way he could reduce costs significantly in his plant in any 90-day period. However, his habit of laying off employees at the end of the year created such ill will among the work force that the plant was plagued by a militant union, higher labor costs, and lower levels of overall productivity. Despite these long-term negative consequences, this plant manager felt driven to make his short-term performance numbers (even though he *knew* it was against the long-term interests of his company).

At Citibank in the late 1970s, Walter Wriston set a growth objective of 15 percent per year—a level of superior performance that Wriston thought his organization was capable of achieving and sustaining. During that period, the competitive environment had changed, and executives went to great lengths to make the 15 percent growth number, even though doing so may have jeopardized the overall health of some of Citibank's businesses. Even today, some would argue that Citibank's culture stresses the accomplishment of short-term financial targets rather than longer-term strategic objectives. (In fairness, it should be noted that Walter Wriston was the CEO who had the guts and foresight to tolerate years of losses while investing in Citibank's retail banking business. Today, this retail business represents a significant competitive advantage for the bank.)

Another common example of the "making the numbers" strategy trap is provided by a small consulting firm we have worked with, which holds its sales representatives strictly accountable for ambitious annual sales targets. The firm has articulated a strategy that places a premium on building strong client relationships. Their sales representatives take pride in working closely with their customers. Yet at the end of each year, these same sales representatives—to make their year-end numbers—aggressively try to sell so hard and so fast that they often weaken the very relationships that the company's strategy exalts. Perhaps, if the firm were less concerned with making the numbers each year, it could focus more effectively on the source of its competitive advantage—its strong client franchise.

Driving managers to make the numbers is always an imperfect method of measuring the success of a strategy, unless the numbers have been carefully constructed to reflect the true ends or objectives. The ultimate purpose of strategy is to win—to achieve above-average results over a sustained period of time. A fixation on annual financial targets ignores (and sometimes even conflicts with) the accomplishment of strategic ends. There are four reasons why "making the numbers" is a dangerous way to run the business:

1. Most companies use targets that are derived from available financial reports or financial measurement systems. If they are crudely applied, these targets may or may not accurately represent the currently desired strategic objectives. To the extent that old numbers fail to measure new strategies, "making the numbers" won't work.

2. Most companies use numbers that have been used before. Although this allows for easy comparison with past performance, it may not represent the best way to measure future performance. New strategies often make historical graphs and charts obsolete.

3. Most companies use short-term numbers to measure success. It can be said that the business is run for Wall Street, not for Main Street. However, strategic objectives can seldom be expressed exclusively in terms of short-term financial numbers. For example, it is often necessary to increase investments (and therefore costs) to secure a long-term position as the low-cost producer. Companies that become obsessed with short-term cost cutting seldom reach the low-cost producer position.

4. Numbers (short-term or long-term) seldom capture the intangible aspects of strategic objectives. They are therefore imperfect ways of representing such factors as quality, customer satisfaction, and service excellence.

Whenever we attempt to counsel executives away from the use of short-term numbers, frustration grows rapidly at all levels of the organization. Everyone likes numbers! Bosses like them and use them as a valuable management tool. Subordinates like them and use them as a primary source of performance feedback. Line managers like them because it gives them a track to run on. And staff managers like them because it gives them something to digest, analyze, and write reports about.

Thus, "making the numbers" is one strategy trap that we do not think should be completely avoided. Many benefits are associated with the use of quantitative performance standards. But executives must be more aware of the tendency to emphasize short-term, explicit numbers at the expense of longer-term, less explicit measures of success. "Making the numbers" is not a trap if the financial numbers include long-term, not just short-term, targets. In addition, it is not a trap if qualitative, subjective, or intangible measures of performance are included *along with* financial numbers. Never assume that the numbers (particularly the short-term numbers) are the ultimate measure of success. Take them for what they are: measures of short-term performance. As such, they measure the effect of tactics, not strategies.

6
Managing the Intangibles

O ne of the most challenging aspects of implementing a new strategy is managing the intangible, invisible, and often uncomfortable aspects of organization life. Executives have a healthy respect for tangible phenomena. They like numbers and statistics and concrete measures of success. They like problems they can "sink their teeth into." They like solutions they can "see." The intangible aspects of organization life, however—such as employee values, beliefs, norms, management style, work climate, or corporate culture—leave them slightly bewildered and not terribly excited. Unfortunately, our experience is that some of the greatest obstacles to successful strategy implementation lie in this area of intangibles. Executives who can learn to manage the intangibles will be way ahead of their competitors.

There are three basic strategy traps involved in this soft and fuzzy world of intangible organizational phenomena. The first is the assumption that a good manager can manage any kind of business with any kind of strategy. The second is the tendency to overanalyze strategic issues, rather than just "getting on with it." And the third is the problem of ignoring the corporate culture. (The basic techniques for avoiding these traps and coming to grips with the intangibles in an organization are described in chapter 8.) Our experience tells us that three things have to happen for senior managers to manage the intangibles successfully:

1. Whenever possible, intangibles must be turned into tangibles. Vague generalities, statements of feeling, and so forth, must

be turned into hard numbers, trends, graphs, charts, and explicitly measurable phenomena.

2. Once the intangibles have been made tangible, methods are needed to provide senior executives with concrete progress measures. Nothing is more frustrating for a senior executive than to be told that morale is lousy, then to be talked into spending $500,000 to improve morale, only to be told a year later that morale is still lousy. Ways of measuring and monitoring the intangibles must be employed with confidence if the senior executive is to manage this aspect of the strategy implementation process successfully.

3. Finally, executives must have faith in their instincts. No matter how hard one tries to make the intangible tangible and measure these "invisible" things, there will always be an element of mystery, intuition, and "gut feel" about the intangibles. Senior executives should trust their instincts when it comes to dealing with these strategy traps. Whether it's called charisma or vision, effective business leadership requires a level of intuitive judgement that often makes the difference between success and failure.

Strategy Trap #13:   A Good Athlete Can Run Any Business

We have seen many managers fall into the trap of believing that there is such a thing as a "professional manager" who can manage any kind of business. Executives who fall into this trap often put the wrong people in charge of implementing their strategies, because they fail to appreciate that some strategies require a blend of qualities that are not found in every successful manager. Differentiation strategies, for example, usually work best in the hands of a market-sensitive, creative executive. Cost leadership strategies require more discipline, more structure, and more patience. Matching a manager's style and strategic orientation with the requirements of the business and the business strategy is one of the most important decisions senior executives can make.

This trap is being recognized increasingly in academic circles.

John Kotter (1982, 1985) of the Harvard Business School and Henry Mintzberg (1973, 1983) of McGill University have published widely read books describing the nature of managerial work. They have pointed out how important it is for executives to have a detailed knowledge of their industry and their organization. Both authors have cautioned against the notion that there is a generic professional manager who can successfully manage widely different kinds of businesses. Despite their writings, however, executives continue to search for "good athletes" rather than for leaders with particular skills, experiences, and management styles.

The Pepsi-Cola Company has an elaborate human resource planning process that helps identify many of these intangible aspects of leadership and leadership style. Pepsi considers the quality of its human resources one of its greatest assets and tried to move managers into positions that take advantage of their styles and experience. Looking at the company's recent success in the marketplace, it is not surprising that its two largest domestic beverage company operations are headed by two very different kinds of executives. Robert Dettmer, president of the Pepsi-Cola Bottling Group (PBG), is a meticulous, systematic, and operations-oriented executive. This is highly appropriate for the 10,000-employee organization he runs. PBG is a large manufacturing, distribution, and sales organization that requires careful coordination and discipline. Roger Enrico, president of Pepsi-Cola USA, is an altogether different kind of executive. Enrico believes in what he calls "idea leadership," and he relies on a marketing-oriented, quick-decision, highly responsive style of management. This is perfectly suited to Pepsi-Cola USA, which is basically a marketing organization that deals with Pepsi's diverse group of independent bottlers and franchise owners. Studies of these two organizations have shown that the styles of the two presidents have permeated well down into their organizations. The work atmosphere in PBG is more predictable, measureable, and disciplined, whereas the emphasis in Pepsi-Cola USA is on entrepreneurship, marketing, and new ideas. Both enterprises have successfully implemented strategies that match the leadership styles of their presidents.

Citibank has responded to the problem of matching leadership style and strategy by developing a three-day training program to teach its executives how to avoid the "good athlete can run any business" strategy trap. This program, called Strategic Management Staffing, emphasizes the importance of diagnosing a manager's strategic orientation *before* selecting that manager to run a given business. By means of case studies, video examples, roleplays, and lectures, Citibankers learn how to identify the traits, characteristics, and behaviors that are associated with various strategic orientations. The two basic strategic orientations identified in this program match Michael Porter's (1980) two basic generic strategies: differentiation and cost leadership. The differentiation orientation stresses an *externally oriented* point of view, with an emphasis on flexibility, rapid and confident decision making, new ideas, and creativity. The cost leadership orientation stresses discipline, structure, and control and is largely *internally oriented*.

The Citibank Strategic Management Staffing program also stresses the importance of analyzing an organization's culture and matching the style of the executive with that culture. Implicit in this training program is the assumption that intangibles such as leadership style are important determinants of success. Citibank has learned from past experience that such is the case.

One of the most dramatic examples of trying to match leadership style and strategy was played out in 1985 at Apple Computer. In 1984, Apple decided to compete for the business and professional market for personal computers, which meant going head-to-head with IBM. Two factors—manufacturing efficiency and marketing—became critical to the success of this new strategy. John Scully, Apple's president, was chosen to execute it. Steven Jobs, Apple's chairman, was not. Jobs had championed technology at Apple. His style—widely reported at the time—stressed creativity, personal loyalty, and informality. Though appropriate in the past, it didn't match Apple's new strategy. Scully's style, which placed a greater emphasis on discipline and rational decision making, fit the strategy better.

Another company that has tried hard to deal with the intangible factor of leadership style is Pepsi-Cola International. This division of PepsiCo, Inc., uses a "skills wheel"—adapted from research done by Personnel Decisions, Inc., of Minneapolis—to help executives identify the leadership traits and skills of their subordinates. (The wheel is reproduced in figure 6–1.) Once these leadership skills have been identified, they are matched against the jobs and the business circumstances. Pepsi-Cola International operates in more than 140 countries around the world—and each country requires its own business proposition. In growing its cadre of international managers, PCI executives are very cognizant of the need to match skills and styles with business strategies. The skills wheel has proved to be a practical tool that enables executives to do this while at the same time providing a valuable vehicle for coaching and counseling.

Strategy Trap #14:   Analysis Paralysis

One of the most difficult leadership challenges is deciding when to stop formulating strategy and begin executing it. Although many executives are action-oriented, the computer has increased our fascination with data and our ability to manipulate data. Top management teams now have access to voluminous performance statistics, market research reports, and other business information. In many cases, these data seem to hold senior managers spellbound. Couple this data overload with even more sophisticated techniques of financial analysis and you have the "analysis paralysis" strategy trap—the inability or unwillingness of executives to take decisive action. This trap becomes more dangerous and more prevalent in firms that are committed to a strategy formulation process that requires creation of lengthy and detailed planning documents.

Proctor and Gamble Company has often been accused of "analysis paralysis." Its management style and corporate culture emphasize careful, deliberate decision making. This slow-moving, perfectionist approach worked well in less competitive times; but in the 1980s, P&G is taking a beating. For example, the company test-marketed a rich and chewy Duncan Hines chocolate-chip cookie in Kansas City in early 1983, and the product was a smashing success. Rather than go national immediately, however, P&G analyzed, deliberated, and waited until September 1984. Meanwhile, Nabisco Brands, PepsiCo, and Keebler all brought out competing products. "By the time P&G was ready to roll, other people were already there," recalls a buyer at a large midwestern supermarket chain.

Proctor and Gamble may also have fallen victim to the "analysis

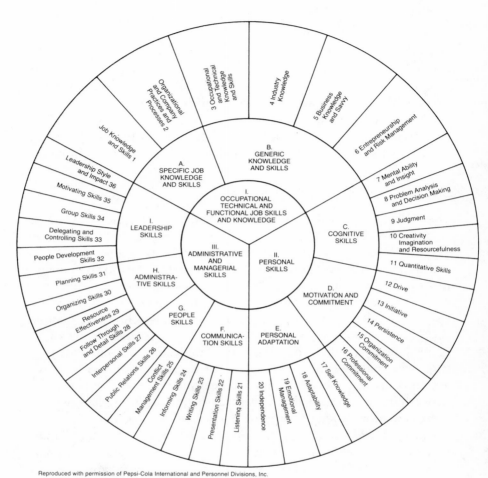

Figure 6–1. *Skills Wheel*

paralysis" trap in its handling of Crest toothpaste. Crest used to dominate Colgate, but Colgate beat P&G to the market with a gel and a pump dispenser. We can't imagine that these innovations were so secret—the difference between Colgate and P&G was that Colgate *moved* and P&G *analyzed.*

Although we are not familiar with the details of the decision— nor do we know how it will eventually turn out—Coca-Cola executives were certainly faced with the "analysis paralysis" dilemma. Their decision to change the flavor of Coke was a courageous one. But consider this: *Time* magazine estimated that nearly 200,000 consumers participated in research that stretched over a 3-year period. Imagine the voluminous market research reports Robert Goizueta, chairman and CEO of Coca-Cola, must have had to study. We're sure the results of many of the studies were equivocal, thus allowing Goizueta and his management team to be trapped by the analysis. Meanwhile, Pepsi continued to gain market share. Finally, on June 10, 1985, Coca-Cola made the historic change.

Unfortunately, the introduction of "new Coke" soon had to be coupled with a reintroduction of "old Coke," and Goizueta's decisiveness was again tested. This time, he avoided the "analysis paralysis" trap. Coca-Cola's willingness to move quickly to correct what *Time* called its "big fizzle" highlights the fact that Goizueta and most of the company's senior managers are "doers" at heart. Their 3-year study of Coke's taste was uncharacteristically mismanaged. The real test of consumer preferences and loyalty was in the marketplace, not in taste-testing research labs. Coca-Cola should have known this. In the soft drink industry, only the "doers" survive.

A final example of a management team falling into the "analysis paralysis" trap was provided by one of our retailing clients. This client, a major retailer with a large department store division, saw new forms of merchandising emerging in the early 1980s. These new forms combined off-price and mass-merchandising techniques. For 3 years, study teams were created, and voluminous amounts of data about the shifting patterns of merchandising were analyzed. But no action was taken. Management couldn't decide whether or not it wanted to be in this line of business. Finally, in 1984, the determination was made to move ahead. It is not surprising that performance has been disappointing, because our client was 3 years late in making its move. Established competitors have proved difficult to dislodge, and our client's share of the market is below acceptable levels.

In the end, executives must trust their instincts. They often must implement strategies with incomplete knowledge of the market, of costs, or of competitive responses. We think this drive to implement strategy sooner (rather than later) makes companies more innovative because it helps limit the "homerun philosophy" of investments, whereby every investment must meet unrealistically high return-on-investment and volume requirements (i.e., must be a homerun). Implementing strategies quickly leads to increased experimentation and allows the company to place more frequent (and smaller) bets. These characteristics match what Gordon Pinchot (1985) calls an "intrapreneurial" environment. Both Pinchot and Peter Drucker (1985) write eloquently about the need to manage the intangible factors in organizations so that new ideas and creativity will flourish. They conclude that avoiding the "analysis paralysis" strategy trap is one sure-fire way to stimulate entrepreneurial innovation and investment.

A final word is necessary about trusting to instinct in implementing strategy. The "analysis paralysis" trap basically involves executives who fail to act. However, we have also observed senior managers who act precipitously—who change strategy at the first sign of trouble and fail to recognize the difference between a temporary market adjustment and a long-term shift in competitive dynamics. Japanese businessmen have often said that their American counterparts are too quick to change their strategies—that they give up too soon. Many times, relying too much on intuition and instinct leads to the opposite of "analysis paralysis"—a variation of the trap that we call "panic management."

"Panic management" characterized a small, privately held company we recently studied. This company, which invested heavily in talented people to differentiate itself, would periodically examine its cost structure and panic. What followed was labeled "Black Friday"—every two years, senior management fired a dozen or so people—always on a Friday afternoon. After these disruptive layoffs, the company (because it appreciated its source of competitive advantage) slowly but surely hired more talented people. We're not sure why its top managers seemed to panic about labor costs every 24 to 30 months, but we heard an executive explain (before one of the "Black Fridays") that he "knew instinctively" that the firm had too many people.

Trusting to instinct shouldn't mean shooting from the hip. Most executives, if they lead active and outgoing lives, analyze *more* data than they need to make high-quality strategic decisions. These data must be organized and systematically applied to a disciplined strategy formulation process to lead to decisive action—action without panic.

In addition to the tools for avoiding strategy traps that are presented in Part III of this book, there are a few commonsense ways to decide when to stop thinking and start acting. We have developed four criteria to help managers avoid "analysis paralysis" and decide when to execute a strategy:

1. Strategies should not be implemented until there is a "critical mass" of managers who have "signed up" for it. Without this critical mass, the new strategy will probably be poorly executed. With it, you can execute with confidence that the organization—and other managers—will fall in line.

2. The timing of strategy implementation sometimes depends on a "window of opportunity." This can be caused by a technological breakthrough, a competitor's blunder, the emergence of a new customer group, or the recognition of an unmet market need. When the cost of *not* implementing is higher than the cost of implementing in error, it's time to execute.

3. Execution of a strategy should begin when the momentum of the organization demands execution. There will be times when it is harder to stand still than to move ahead. When such times arise, use the building momentum to get off to a fast start with the new strategy. Holding the organization

back at this stage is seldom advisable. It should go without saying that moving ahead without this organizational momentum is also inadvisable.

4. Strategies should not be executed without implementation plans. At a minimum, an implementation plan should contain the following elements:

   - Key strategic targets should be identified and clearly described.

   - Major actions and initiatives should be specified and delegated to key people or groups.

   - Revenue, cost, and profit parameters for all new initiatives should be identified, and specific accountabilities should be created for these parameters. (In creating these parameters, executives must avoid the "making the numbers" trap. Quantitative targets must be flexible when implementing a new strategy.)

   - A communications plan for the new strategy should be agreed to and accepted by the top management team.

   - Sources of potential resistance to the new strategy should be identified, and steps for overcoming this resistance should be made explicit. (Don't trust to luck here.)

   - Timetables, milestones, and contingency plans should be developed. These should cover at least the coming year and should apply to at least the top management team.

If none of these four criteria is met, further strategic analysis and planning are necessary, because your strategy is not ready to be implemented. If all four criteria are met, go ahead and push the button—your strategy should be executed immediately. If only two or three of the criteria are met, or if there are questions about any of the criteria, execution can proceed, but you should expect implementation difficulties. Proceed with caution. You may be avoiding the "analysis paralysis" strategy trap but stepping into several others.

Strategy Trap #15:   Ignoring the Corporate Culture

In many ways, this final strategy trap is a summary of all of the implementation strategy traps. In our experience, the single most pervasive implementation problem for senior managers is ignoring their own corporate culture. Time and time again, we have seen managers who are brilliant in creating marketing or business strategies that take advantage of competitive opportunities in the marketplace but ignore the realities and limitations of their own organization. Many times, the strengths and weaknesses of a corporation are not reflected in the balance sheet, the income statement, the product line, the technology, or the tangible representations of corporate assets. Often, an organization's most important resource is the intangible system of values, beliefs, norms, and expectations—which have come to be called the *corporate culture*. If an executive ignores these values, beliefs, and cultural realities when the strategy is formulated, implementing the strategy becomes very difficult.

One of the most dramatic examples of this strategy trap was played out in the late 1970s and early 1980s at AT&T. Rapidly changing technology and decontrol of the communications industry lead AT&T to modify its strategy and emphasize proactive marketing and aggressive salesmanship. Arch McGill was brought in from IBM to reformulate and implement this new strategy. For 3 years, he struggled with various business problems, but none proved so difficult to solve as the problem of changing AT&T's corporate culture. We had firsthand experience with AT&T during this transition period. Despite thousands of hours of training, the replacement of hundreds of managers, and the repeated exhortations of senior managers, AT&T was unable to take full advantage of its new marketing initiatives. Arch McGill himself admitted that the problem was "cultural." (It should be noted that this term was not widely used back in 1978, when McGill was struggling with AT&T's new strategic direction.) It proved almost impossible to convince long-time AT&T managers and employees that customer service was *not* the only goal of the telephone company. The value of customer service had been so ingrained in that organization that McGill, despite herculian efforts, was unable to substitute new values, such as technological innovation, market responsiveness, and (for commercial customers) solving business problems.

We're not sure what Arch McGill could have done differently at AT&T to implement its new strategy more effectively, but one lesson stands out. If your organization's business strategy depends on having employees behave in a certain way, you'd better have the basic fabric or culture of that organization carefully aligned and in tune with those required behaviors. Failing to line up the corporate culture with the strategy dooms the strategy. Culture will win out every time.

One business leader who understood this lesson was Bob Lipp, now one of the presidents of the Chemical New York Corporation. Back in 1982, when Lipp was in charge of the retail banking group, he proved to be a master of culture management. A dynamic leader in his own right, he usually coupled changes in business strategy with a comprehensive and systematic public relations campaign that attempted to aggressively manage the intangible aspects of Chemical Bank's internal organization. For example, Lipp masterminded a series of retail banking commercials that stressed the importance of delivering high-quality customer service. These advertisements were aimed unabashedly at the employees of the bank, not the customers. Lipp correctly identified employee attitudes as the major barrier to the delivery of high-quality customer service. By clearly portraying in these advertisements what it was like to deliver high-quality service, he established a model and vision for his own organization. Over a period of 18 months he was able to improve the bank's market position and begin to change the corporate culture at the bank. Customer service became one of the most important values for that organization.

Why do executives fall into the "ignoring the corporate culture" trap? In many cases, senior managers are simply unaware of their organization's culture. It is, after all, a very subtle—almost invisible—feature of the company. Made up of the general ambience, attitudes, traditions, corporate mythologies and legends, and a host of other factors, the culture is written down nowhere but exists everywhere within the organization. In other cases, managers overestimate the organization's ability to adapt to a new strategy. In still others, the senior executives are part of the problem. They have built successful organizations and do not want to tear down and re-create their corporate cultures, even when a new strategy is adopted. Whether because of ignorance, optimism, defensiveness, or (in many cases) just plain stubborness, the difficulties experienced by companies in adjusting their corporate cultures to new business strategies have created a very profitable environment for consulting firms. During the past 2 years alone, five major corporations have sought our assistance in this area. In addition, companies such as the Management Analysis Center, McKinsey and Company, The Delta Group, and The Forum Corporation have all been active and effective as culture management partners to big business.

A Case Study: Managing the Culture at Pepsi

One of the most ambitious culture management projects we have been involved in is with the Pepsi-Cola Company. For the past 3 years, we have helped Pepsi manage an important shift in its corporate culture. This shift has allowed the company to execute a series of new business strategies and has provided us with important insights into the process of managing corporate culture.

The Need for Culture Change at Pepsi

The Pepsi-Cola Company experienced dramatic growth during the 1970s. Sales grew over 10 percent per year, and Pepsi became the largest-selling soft drink in the American supermarket. One of the causes of this growth was the enormously successful "Pepsi Challenge" advertising campaign, which highlighted the taste differential of Pepsi over Coke. By 1982, Coca-Cola was retaliating with even more aggressive price discounting. Pepsi-Cola met this discounting by increasing its promotional spending and reducing its own prices. Margins shrank and volume growth slowed. These competitive developments were all the more worrisome to Pepsi-Cola executives, because Seven-Up, a brand that had always been a distant third in the market, was now owned by the Philip Morris Company, a strong consumer goods marketer.

The need for a modified business strategy was emphasized by PepsiCo's corporate strategic planners. Led by McKinsey-trained Andrall Pearson, PepsiCo strategists had developed more sophisticated planning techniques and methodologies. They realized that primary demand for cola-flavored soft drinks in 1981 and 1982 grew at a rate of less than 4 percent per year. By 1983, the diet and caffeine-free segments accounted for most of the growth in the market.

Pepsi's response to these developments was to shift its strategy and modify its business definition. In 1983, executives began to refer to the company as a "refreshment beverage company," not a soft drink (or perhaps more accurate, a cola) company. This broader business definition increased Pepsi's growth options and opportunities. In addition, senior management made the following decisions:

1. Greater emphasis was to be placed on new product development and product innovation.

2. Cost controls and productivity improvements were to be stressed to protect profit margins in the face of continued price competition from Coca-Cola.

3. Independent bottlers were to receive increased attention, and expansion of company-owned bottling operations was to be more selective.

These new strategic priorities placed new demands on the Pepsi organization. Stimulated by years of rapid growth of the company-owned bottling group, managers had expected to be promoted rapidly. Now, they would be expected to stay in their jobs for longer periods of time. High mobility and the successes of the late 1970s had created a culture that stressed short-term results. Now, the requirement was for a longer-term perspective as the company attempted to introduce new products and reposition old ones. Finally, the new strategy placed a premium on management, whereas in the past, Pepsi executives had tended to emphasize marketing and selling. Now, skills such as goal setting, coaching, and delegating were recognized as critical if cost controls, productivity improvements, and improved bottler relations were to be achieved.

Although Pepsi's shift in business strategy was the major force driving culture change, there was a growing realization that the organization had grown too large and too complex to be managed "in the same old way." The number of exempt personnel doubled from 1978 to 1983. The average age of senior managers dropped from 49 to 41 during this same period, and the company added four new sales and marketing groups. Decision making was made more difficult, communications were becoming strained, and managers—though less seasoned and less experienced—were required to execute new and even more challenging strategies.

The need to modify the Pepsi-Cola corporate culture was also highlighted by attitude surveys conducted in 1982 and 1983. Results of these surveys showed that although most managers found Pepsi an exciting and dynamic place to work, many managers felt that the company devoted insufficient time and attention to personal development. The culture was characterized by a "sink or swim," "up or out" philosophy that needed to be changed if Pepsi was going to meet the expectations of its younger, better educated staff and attract and retain *managers,* not just *marketers.*

Finally, the need for change at Pepsi stemmed from the culture itself. Executives took pride in being results-oriented and successful. One of the most common phrases heard in the company's corporate headquarters in Purchase, New York, was "Make it happen." It is not surprising, therefore, that lower-than-expected performance would be followed by thorough reexamination of the factors that contributed to the disappointing results. As one Pepsi-Cola executive explained in January 1983:

> We're not looking to radically change the culture that has helped us "win" in the marketplace. But, we must modify some of our priorities. We must become more of a career company; we must become better people managers and better coaches; we must look to longer term results; and above all, we must not lower our standards.

Pepsi's Approach to Culture Management

Led by Michael C. Feiner, vice-president of personnel, Pepsi's approach involved three initiatives. First, the issue of culture management was made explicit and clear. Before 1983, it was considered "soft" to discuss people management and corporate culture. By 1984, executives at all levels were openly describing, debating, and discussing the Pepsi-Cola corporate culture.

Second, Pepsi chose to use training as a major culture management tool. Under the guidance of Bruce Saari, Pepsi's director of management development, the company developed a 3½-day leadership workshop and put 200 of its most senior managers through the program. More than 10,000 hours of executive time were devoted to discussing the old-versus-the-new Pepsi and to learning techniques for personal success, for helping others succeed, and for managing the culture more effectively. More than anything else, this commitment to training helped convince managers that the company was serious about changing its culture.

A unique feature of Pepsi's training was its use of confidential surveys that allowed each participant to evaluate his or her leadership. Feiner, Saari, and Hilary Eaton, Pepsi's training manager, developed a preliminary list of "executive leadership practices" that described how Pepsi managers should behave in the new culture. This list of management behaviors was carefully reviewed by all of Pepsi-Cola's top executives. They modified the practices to match the needs of each of their business units and, in the process, defined a *model* of effective leadership that was uniquely suited to Pepsi-Cola. This list of leadership practices, shown in figure 6–2, was turned into a survey instrument so that Pepsi managers could receive confidential reports on their use of the practices. (Survey results were shown only to program participants; they were not seen by others at Pepsi.)

The third Pepsi-Cola initiative involved managing key personnel management systems. Three systems were modified to encourage new leadership behavior and support the desired culture:

1. Pepsi's human resources planning (HRP) process was expanded to include one-on-one "developmental feedback" ses-

EXECUTIVE LEADERSHIP PROGRAM

A Program Designed To Build Managerial Excellence

GAINING A STRATEGIC PERSPECTIVE	BUILDING A LONG-TERM COMMITMENT TO EXCELLENCE	DEMONSTRATING A RESPONSIVE LEADERSHIP STYLE	CREATING A CLIMATE OF INDIVIDUAL RESPONSIBILITY	COACHING FOR RESULTS	ESTABLISHING A NETWORK FOR SUCCESS
Market Knowledge 1. Staying abreast of changing industry and market conditions 2. Being aware of competitors' strengths and weaknesses 3. Understanding the critical "leverage points" of the business **Business Priorities** 4. Establishing functional priorities that reflect the long-term needs of the business 5. Helping subordinates understand the tradeoffs between NOPAT, SOM, Volume and ROAE 6. Helping subordinates focus on the bottom line impact of decisions, projects or programs	**High Standards** 7. Establishing high performance goals and standards for subordinates 8. Consistently demonstrating high levels of integrity in your daily contacts with others 9. Relating rewards to excellence of performance, rather than to other factors (such as personal relationships) **Continuity** 10. Solving immediate problems without sacrificing long-term results 11. Managing change in a thoughtful and well planned manner rather than a reactive manner 12. Selecting the right people to staff the organization	**Interpersonal Flexibility** 13. Being willing to change one's management emphasis as the needs of the business/function change 14. Dealing effectively with multiple priorities and many conflicting issues 15. Encouraging new ideas and alternative points of view **Decisiveness** 16. Being willing to make tough decisions in implementing plans 17. Being willing to speak out on issues, even when your view is unpopular 18. Confronting conflict situations in an honest and direct manner 19. Giving subordinates a clear-cut decision when they need one	**Delegation** 20. Giving subordinates the opportunity to influence the setting of individual and departmental goals 21. Being clear and thorough in delegating responsibilities 22. Expecting subordinates to find and correct their own errors rather than doing this for them **Entrepreneurship** 23. Encouraging innovation and calculated risk taking 24. Encouraging entrepreneurial behavior by avoiding excessive controls 25. Recognizing subordinates for good performance more than criticizing them for performance problems	**Supportiveness** 26. Being supportive and helpful in contacts with subordinates 27. Going to bat for subordinates when you feel they are right **Constructive Feedback** 28. Being open and candid in dealings with people rather than being vague and indirect 29. Working constructively with subordinates to correct performance problems 30. Explaining the rationale for decisions that are made **Career Management** 31. On an ongoing basis, coaching subordinates on how to succeed at Pepsi 32. Considering subordinates' needs when making career decisions	**Contacts** 33. Maintaining a broad circle of contacts throughout PepsiCo. 34. Using contacts outside PepsiCo to accomplish your objectives 35. Using informal channels to collect information and achieve business objectives **Collaboration** 36. Working effectively with people in other departments or functions 37. Encouraging subordinates to collaborate with other departments or functions

Reproduced with permission of Pepsi-Cola Company.

Figure 6–2. *Pepsi's Executive Leadership Practices List*

sions between managers and subordinates. Beginning in the summer of 1984, bosses were required to provide annual feedback on each subordinate's skills and abilities. These sessions increased both the quantity and the quality of dialogue at Pepsi and helped reinforce the new culture's emphasis on people development.

2. The HRP system was also changed to encourage employees to stay in their jobs for longer periods of time. Each year, Pepsi's senior managers developed detailed "game plans" for their organization. Those game plans now stressed the importance of stability and continuity, rather than the traditional "up or out" philosophy. This increased the emphasis on on-the-job coaching of underperformers, rather than replacing them with new people.

3. Pepsi's performance appraisal system for managers was modified to include people management goals as well as the traditional measures of performance.

Pepsi's Success
It's too early to measure the success of Pepsi-Cola's culture management project. Initial results are encouraging, however. Managers at all levels report that the environment has become more supportive. Turnover has decreased, and climate surveys conducted in 1985 show that many parts of the organization are healthier than they were in 1982 and 1983. It is not surprising that bottom-line results have steadily improved.

It remains to be seen whether or not the long-term impact of the Pepsi-Cola culture management experience will allow this organization to meet its strategic objectives. What we do know is that without these initiatives, performance would have suffered. The "cola war" continues; Pepsi and Coke compete on all fronts—for market share, management talent, public image, and brand loyalty. Pepsi-Cola views its corporate culture as a long-term source of competitive advantage, and the company has devoted significant time and energy to managing this culture.

Pepsi's experience is not unique. Culture management requires the commitment of substantial resources and a level of patience that is not always found at the senior levels of most organizations. Many of the lessons we have learned at PepsiCo are incorporated into the techniques we present for managing corporate culture (chapter 8) and for managing strategic change (chapter 9). Certainly, none of these techniques will *guarantee* success, but they will provide managers with a useful framework for managing the intangible, "fuzzy," hard-to-control aspects of the organization.

Part III
Tools for Avoiding Strategy Traps

In Parts I and II of this book we have suggested many ways for managers to avoid being caught in strategy traps. We believe that the key to avoiding the formulation traps is to use a Commonsense Approach to creating the strategy. Similarly, the key to avoiding the implementation traps is for executives to demonstrate a more sensitive and more enlightened brand of business leadership.

In Part III, our recommendations for avoiding strategy traps are expanded and organized into three different strategy-building and strategy implementation tools. We've used these tools with great success in our consulting practice. Chapter Seven outlines a process model for formulating strategy. This model not only encourages high quality strategic thinking, but enables executive teams to creatively participate in developing the strategic plan.

Once a strategy has been successfully formulated, there are still a number of traps to be avoided. Chapter 8 describes a process for managing the intangible forces that often prevent organizations from achieving their objectives.

The organizational climate system outlined in this chapter allows executives to measure and control these forces. Finally, Chapter 9 is devoted to the problem of overcoming resistance to strategic change. Effective strategy implementation often depends on an executive's ability to mobilize the organization and motivate people to do things differently. Twelve practical management techniques for managing change and implementing strategy are described.

7

How to Do Strategic Planning

We have already acknowledged that there is no "perfect" strategy-building process. Success in formulating and executing strategy depends on a combination of intellectual, interpersonal, and leadership factors, and there is no simple formula that will work for every business. However, every business should have a strategic plan—a document, however brief, that describes the long-term vision and mission of the business and defines how the company will "win." No activity is more important to good strategy building than the creation of this document.

The development of a strategic plan is not an attempt to predict the future. Rather, it is a way of determining the realistic directions a company can pursue, where it should go, and how it can get there. In short, it is a way of *creating* the future.

A strategic plan is like the rudder on a sailboat. Without a rudder, the sailboat will drift aimlessly or will be carried along by the wind. It will do no good to take continual readings of the wind or current to rechart its position—the boat will still drift out of control. Yet with a rudder, a little wind, and—most important—a skilled sailor to set and hold the course, the boat will go in the direction toward which it is set. Its performance will be both planned and controlled. The key to sound strategic planning, then, is to ensure that the "rudder" is in shape, in place, and properly set before the journey begins. What does this suggest as the function of a plan?

Adapted with permission from material copyrighted by Harbridge House, Inc., Boston, MA.

First, a strategic plan should serve as a tool—to assess the true position and capability of the company, to identify developing and potential opportunities, to devise an advantageous competitive position, and to determine specifically what must be done to execute a particular strategy.

Second, a strategic plan should consider long-range policy issues in time to permit timely initiation of long-lead-time activities. Such an approach is a requirement for survival in industries where the replenishment of certain resources must be decided 3, 5, or even 10 years before they actually affect corporate performance.

Third, a strategic plan should provide a framework or focal point for all of the organization's activities, uniting hundreds of employees, dozens of departments, and any number of strong-willed managers so that they *all* move in the same direction at the same time and reach the agreed-upon goals despite problems and obstacles that arise along the way.

Fourth, and perhaps most important, a strategic plan should force top management to come to grips with what the company is and to determine where it can and should go as well as what actions—and sacrifices—may be necessary to get it there. The kind of management agreement and commitment required here is often assumed to exist when, in fact, it rarely does.

Most top managers spend a surprising amount of their time talking about these kinds of issues and about their company's prospects, competitors, problems, and opportunities. But this talking usually takes place before formal meetings—over cocktails and in other informal situations. Such conversations are often useful in dealing with tactical issues, but they don't lead to a usable strategic plan. By definition, informal discussion lacks the logical framework or the kind of step-by-step, building-block process that, though somewhat mechanical, is necessary for developing a workable planning document.

Developing a Strategic Plan

A strategic plan is usually developed according to a carefully laid out set of sequential decision-making steps—a planning model. We outlined the framework of a highly effective planning model—our

"Commonsense Approach" to formulating strategy—in the introduction to Part I. This four-step process is streamlined enough to be used by line executives yet comprehensive enough to produce high-quality strategic plans. The expanded version of our Commonsense Approach presented in figure 7–1 illustrates all of the critical issues senior managers must come to grips with in formulating a winning strategy.

This model describes the intellectual part of strategic planning. *Using* the model effectively requires combining the intellectual process with the right kinds of interpersonal and leadership processes. Strategic plans should be developed by the senior managers who run the business. Planning conferences involving groups of a dozen or so executives are the best way to integrate our Commonsense Approach with the participative methods necessary for good strategy building. Such conferences should be limited to senior managers who have a genuine stake in the business. If there are too many managers, the conference become unwieldy; if there are too few, key decision makers are excluded and important information is missing.

Consultants should be used to guide the process but not to *do* the actual planning. We have developed a highly effective system for facilitating such strategic planning conferences. We use the model shown in figure 7–1 as the working agenda; this provides the required intellectual discipline. The executive team should have time to prepare for the conference and familiarize themselves with the planning model. The conference itself is usually divided into two segments, sometimes separated by two or three weeks. The initial segment, which lasts a day or two, focuses on the first half of the planning model (up to the development of objectives). The final segment, which normally lasts a day, deals with the last half of the model. Detailed action planning need not be done in the group setting, which is why the segments are often separated by several weeks.

The balance of this chapter will describe the components of the planning model. Although our description may sound somewhat mechanical or theoretical, it is important to remember that each step of the process involves a dozen senior managers analyzing, discussing, and debating the issues. Developing a good strategic plan should be anything but mechanical or theoretical.

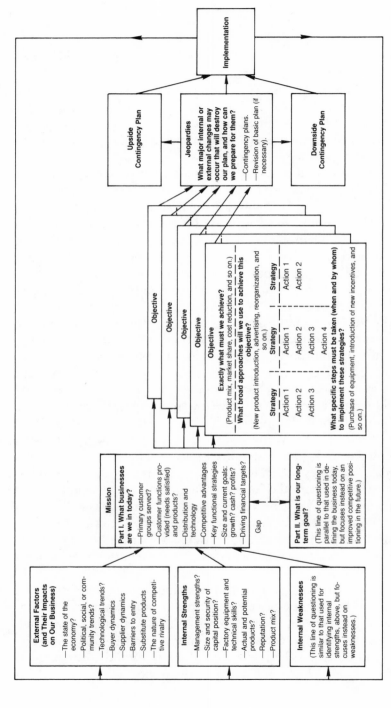

Figure 7–1. *A Strategic Planning Model*

External Factors and Internal Strengths and Weaknesses: Considerations in Developing the Mission

The first basic step in the strategic planning process—development of the mission—cannot be undertaken without first giving careful consideration to both external influences and internal capabilities.

External Factors

The external factors to be considered are the forces and currents outside the organization. Managers too often tend to assume that society and the economy will continue to support their businesses more or less as they have in the past. This is clearly not a valid assumption. Accordingly, any consideration of external influences must include an analysis of a wide range of factors, such as buyer power, potential entrants, supplier power, the state of the economy, the actual and anticipated programs of the competition, and the life and values of the communities in which the business operates.

Michael Porter's (1980) model of industry analysis provides a useful framework for analyzing the external environment. His model, as presented in his book *Competitive Strategy,* examines the competitive forces operating in the external environment. Each industry, Porter argues, has its own dynamic, which ultimately determines its profitability. Moreover, this dynamic sets the stage for and influences the profitability of each firm competing in the industry. This dynamic can be analyzed by assessing (1) the power of buyers and how this power varies among buyer groups (Porter uses the term *power* to represent the ability and willingness of buyer groups to negotiate for lower prices or more quality/services— requiring higher costs—from suppliers); (2) the power of suppliers; (3) the power of potential entrants to the industry; (4) the power of substitute products/services for those that the industry offers; and (5) the power of rivalry among firms. Each of these power sources operates to reduce industry and firm profitability. Over time, in the absence of an effective strategy, these power sources will erode the firm's competitive advantage.

Each external factor must be clearly identified, and its impact on the business must be defined. For example, it would be insufficient to say that government is a key external influence on your business. It would be more useful to describe the factor as follows:

Factor: The number of government regulations that require compliance reporting is proliferating.

Impact: Increased paperwork and longer lead times on capital projects.

Internal Strengths and Weaknesses

In contrast to the external influences that exist *outside* the walls of an organization, the internal strengths and weaknesses are all of the raw materials a company has to work with—its assets, capital, actual and potential products, reputation, managerial capability, factory equipment, and technical skills. Strengths and weaknesses should be listed separately to ensure that strengths are fully leveraged and weaknesses are either addressed or accepted. Remember that strengths, in Porter's terminology, are potential sources of sustainable competitive advantage for the firm. Weaknesses include what is missing in terms of competitive advantage.

In his book *Competitive Advantage,* Porter (1985) provides a useful framework for assessing a firm's internal strengths and weaknesses. He argues that the organization should be broken up into the major activities that provide value for its customers (e.g., procuring raw materials, manufacturing, marketing, postsale service). Porter calls this sequence of activities the firm's "value chain." By carefully analyzing the value chain, potential sources of competitive advantage (or disadvantage) can be identified.

If an organization is to determine accurately where it can go, it must be able to determine honestly what raw materials, or building blocks, it has. Most companies have assets and liabilities that are unrecognized and therefore are not properly positioned. A value chain analysis will help identify a firm's real strengths and weaknesses. A good deal of objectivity is required to assess these raw materials and to envision an organizational structure that utilizes them properly. However, this kind of candor, insight, and creativity can mean the difference between survival and failure. Brutal honesty in this segmentof the plan provides a vital foundation for what is to follow.

The Mission

After looking closely at both the external factors and the internal strengths and weaknesses, it is possible to develop the company's mission. The mission statement is the pivotal segment of the strategic plan in that it determines the scope of all future activity. It is intended to do the following:

1. State explicitly current assumptions and values that were previously unstated.

2. Force reappraisal of traditional assumptions about the nature of the business.

3. Stimulate creativity regarding future directions.

4. Force confrontation and resolution of "gut" issues.

5. Define a strategic gap between the business as it exists today and the business as it will exist at the end of the planning period. Are there new customer groups to be served, new products or services to be offered, new technologies or new channels of distribution to be utilized? These and other gaps in the definition of the business must be made explicit.

The definition of a company's mission should be sufficiently broad and clear to include not only what the company is doing now but also what it may reasonably be expected to do in the future.

The mission statement is developed in two parts through the use of two general questions: "What business are we in today?" and "What is our long-term goal?" The first question, "What business are we in today?"—that is, "What is our current business definition?"—is answered in a few pages and describes the following factors:

1. The *primary customer groups* served by the company: This is intended to force managers to segment their markets and to differentiate among customer groups currently served and those not currently served.

2. *Customer functions and products* provided: This focuses on the product and on the need that is being satisfied when the customer buys the product. For example, is the customer buying reliability? Convenience? Speed? Bare-bones product operation? Ego fulfillment?

3. *Distribution and technology* used to provide the customer functions and products to the primary groups served by the firm: This critical component of strategy requires that the manager examine whether the distribution and technology are consistent with the functions and products. How a firm selects targeted customer groups, customer functions, and distribution/technology can be a source of competitive advantage or disadvantage. For example, broadening the targeted groups, functions, and distribution may provide economies of scale, but at the expense of organization coherence, whereas being too focused on any of these dimensions may leave a firm vulnerable to competitive firms whose offer includes a "one-stop shop."

4. *Key functional policies* that support the business definition: At a minimum, management information systems and personnel, financial control, and marketing policies should be included.

5. *Competitive advantages* that the business has to allow it to win today.

6. *Size and current goals*—growth, cash, profits: The broad financial expectations for a company determine many of its operating priorities. A company that is seeking rapid growth may sacrifice short-term profits to invest in future growth by means of research, product development, market development, and so on. In contrast, a company that is seeking to be a cash generator will avoid most investments and will seek to

use the business to throw off cash and profits. Finally, a company that is seeking current earnings is likely to limit its investment to those activities that are essential to support a continued earnings flow.

7. *Driving financial targets*: The few financial targets that are most important in achieving the company's basic goals drive management decision making. For example, a company that is driving for market share would be likely to accept price reductions rather than lose a major order to a competitor. Generally, targets include market share, sales dollars, unit volume, net income, and return on investment.

This "today" statement should be expressed in realistic terms. It should accurately portray the business as it currently exists so that a constrasting future statement can be constructed.

The second question—"What is our long-term goal?"—is answered by a statement intended to represent an improved competitive positioning for the company in terms of the same factors identified as part of the "today" mission statement. After considering the external forces that affect the company and its internal strengths and weaknesses, the company's executives define a *more advantageous* combination of customer groups, customer functions, ways of delivering customer functions, new "driving" goals, primary financial targets for the future, and competitive advantages the firm will have to result in this vision of the business *winning*. Finally, the mission statement should state how the overall strategy of the business will be supported by key functional strategies. By altering the competitive positioning in this way, the "future" statement attempts to define exactly what the company might hope to become if all of its internal resources were used in the best possible way and in full consideration of the constraints and opportunities imposed by external influences. This "future" statement should also be expressed in realistic terms, thereby defining the gap to be filled through the strategic plan.

The combination of the two mission statements determines the fundamental nature and direction of the organization through the planning period. Serious errors can be made if the mission is stated either too narrowly or too broadly. If it is defined too narrowly, it can limit the organization's activities. Managers might not consider valuable opportunities or they might refrain from taking necessary action. Yet the mission must not be so broadly stated that it is meaningless. For example, ITT's former mission statement—"to provide goods and services to peoples and nations everywhere"—was so broad that it permitted a wide range of inappropriate activities in the middle 1970s.

Objectives

Objectives can be developed only after the mission has been defined, because it is impossible to know whether objectives are reasonable or consistent until the kind of business the company is in and its long-term goal have been determined.

Objectives state exactly what *must* be achieved to fill the gap between the "today" mission statement and the "future" mission statement. An objective is a specific, shorter-term, measurable, pragmatic statement that defines a tangible achievement or outcome. The use of the word *must* here—as opposed to *should* or *might*—is significant. It is important in this early stage of strategic planning for everyone involved to agree that certain objectives *must* be achieved—that these objectives are not simply hopeful targets that it would be "nice" to achieve. In addition, each objective must be stated in terms that are precise enough to eliminate disagreement regarding *when* the objective has been achieved.

Normally, we encourage our clients to develop objectives that cover such areas as product mix, market share, costs, and profits, as well as objectives relating to operational improvements, productivity, service, quality, control, and managerial communications or cooperation.

Strategies

Strategies, as we use the term in this planning model, are the broad approaches taken to achieve each of the company's objectives. They form the "guts" of the strategic plan. They are developed after the objectives and are directly dependent on them. Strategies do not exist in isolation from identified objectives, any more than a means exists in isolation from an end.

For example, if a company's objective is to double its market share, it will probably have a number of strategies along the lines of introducing new products, increasing the size of the sales force, and increasing the size of the plant. In contrast, if its objective is to reduce costs by 20 percent, it will probably have to develop strategies to reduce overtime, tighten control of inventories, and eliminate peripheral operations. Thus, strategies are broad, major tasks or approaches that are needed to achieve each objective.

One of the most difficult tasks at this stage of the planning process is to ensure consistency across objectives, particularly as the objectives involve functional priorities or decisions that could conceivably be in conflict with one another. At this point, it is also possible to begin testing the plan by a kind of backward checking process. This entails evaluating the strength and completeness of the strategies against the objectives they are intended to achieve and the validity and appropriateness of the objectives against the mission. For example, we might ask, "If all of these strategies succeed, will the objective be fully achieved?" If the answer is no (and it often is), then either new and better strategies must be devised or the objective must be reduced in scope. Similarly, the objectives can be tested against the mission by asking, "Are the objectives consistent with the mission? With the business that we are in? With our long-term goals?" If the answers again are no, then either the objectives or the mission must be changed.

Action Steps: Details of Implementation

Our thoughts about the minimum requirements for an implementation action plan were outlined in chapter 6 when we described ways to avoid the "analysis paralysis" strategy trap. The action steps are completely dependent on the strategies, because they are specific actions that must be taken to put each strategy into effect. In other words, if the strategy is to introduce new products (for example, in support of an objective to double market share), then specific steps must be taken to introduce the products. Such steps would probably include development of a detailed research schedule, a timetable for product introduction and for filling the ware-houses, and a program for advertising the new products, and any other actions required to bring the products on stream in the marketplace at a profit.

It might be argued that detailed action steps should not be included in the strategic plan. Our experience, however, is that without such short-term, actionable (and tactical) guidelines, strategic plans are seldom *used*. Implementation is sporadic and sloppy unless long-term goals are translated into short-term actions.

Jeopardies and Contingency Plans

Identification of jeopardies is perhaps the least understood portion of the strategic planning process. As one of the last major steps in developing the basic written plan, jeopardies are identified after the action steps have been set forth. In identifying jeopardies, managers ask, "What major internal or external events—either positive or negative—may occur that will destroy our plan?"

One might wonder whether such a line of questioning might weaken the commitment needed to carry out the plan. Although this is certainly a legitimate concern, it is important to recognize that even the best of strategic plans can and will be destroyed if certain events occur in the economy, in the industry, or, conceivably, within the company. Therefore, it would be foolhardy not to think through such possibilities and prepare contingency plans for the most probable and significant ones.

A contingency plan identifies the specific circumstances that would cause the plan to be activated and outlines the steps the business would take if an extraordinarily good or bad set of events were to occur. Contingency plans are usually short and general; they do not approach the level of sophistication or detail of the basic strategic plan. However, they are important because they indicate the actions that are needed to respond to conceivable events that could make the basic plan invalid.

Management teams frequently react poorly in times of crisis, and decisions made during such periods are generally weak. Therefore, it is far better to prepare contingency plans in an atmosphere of calm and reason, rather than waiting for a crisis to occur and being forced to plan under the most emotional and strained circumstances.

Contingency plans are usually considered necessary only in preparation for a "bad" event. However, a "good" event can also cause problems. For example, if sales suddenly doubled, this would be a fortuitous event, but most manufacturing companies would lack sufficient raw materials, equipment, and warehouse space to handle such a good event. Accordingly, contingency plans are often developed on both an "upside" and "downside" basis; that is, the company plans for economic, market, or competitive situations that are both far better (upside) and far worse (downside) than it actually anticipates.

Implementation

Once the basic steps of the planning process have been discussed, debated, agreed upon, and documented, the final plan is almost complete. Before implementation begins, however, the strategic plan should be reviewed to ensure that the action steps set forth clearly and specifically *what* is to be done, by *whom*, and *when*. Such benchmarks provide reference points for determining whether the plan is on target (time, cost, etc.) and whether stated objectives are being met.

Some type of control system must be established to monitor performance and to trigger reaction when specific tasks and milestones are not being met. Benchmarks and the system of control that surrounds them are extraordinarily important, yet they are often handled very poorly. This means that some individual or group should be assigned to monitor progress against the overall plan.

The next step is to put the plan into action—to put it to work in the real operating world where day-to-day decisions are made—and to determine through the company's actual performance whether or not the strategic plan is valid.

Making the Strategic Plan an Operating Plan

The planning model we have described combines long-range and short-term planning. If such plans are systematically tied to the annual budget, they can become true operating plans, and as such, they must be kept current. How often, then, should a company change its strategic plan?

Over a short period of time, there is less change in the beginning steps of the plan than in the concluding ones. For example, the mission of a company generally changes infrequently, whereas objectives may change over a 1- to 3-year period, and strategies and action steps usually change each year because even with the same basic objectives, the means and approaches by which they are to be achieved have to be revised. Jeopardies also tend to change frequently, particularly when the industry or political climate is in a state of flux.

Given the normal levels of change that can be expected, most strategic plans should be updated at least annually—more often in particularly dynamic or difficult situations. To ensure that a strategic plan is properly updated, a mechanism for updating—including a procedure, a timetable, and assignment of responsibility—must be explicitly set out as part of the basic planning process. This is the only way to ensure that the strategic plan can continue to function as an operating plan.

Summary

This chapter has attempted to counter the common fallacy that increasingly complicated problems require increasingly complicated solutions. The planning model we have described is not difficult to use. Groups of a dozen or so senior managers, if properly guided, can work their way through the entire process in two to three days. Such an investment, rather than being extravagant, is a remarkably modest price to pay for the vision, insight, and commitment that can be generated when the process is done right.

8
How to Manage Corporate Culture

To execute a new business strategy successfully, executives frequently must change the ways in which their managers operate. They have to manage the intangibles of their organization more and more, which is referred to as changing the corporate culture. As noted in chapter 6, we have been actively involved in helping many of our clients come to grips with the problem of managing the intangible, "cultural" aspects of their business organizations. This chapter summarizes what we have learned about changing corporate cultures and outlines a step-by-step approach that can be used to help senior managers implement strategy.

What Is Corporate Culture?

Corporate culture can be divided into five components: values, beliefs, myths, traditions, and norms. *Values* are the ways in which employees assess certain traits, qualities, activities, or behaviors as good or bad, productive or wasteful. High levels of customer service, for example, might be a core value of a particular organization. This value might be reflected in such things as the company motto, measurement systems that focus on response time and reliability, the proportion and seniority of the staff who are available

Adapted with permission from material copyrighted by Harbridge House, Inc., Boston, MA.

to respond to customer questions and complaints, or the frequency with which senior executives comment on dedication to ensuring quality service.

Beliefs, though frequently unstated, reflect people's understanding of the way the organization works and the probable consequences of the actions they take. For example, in some organizations, people champion new product ideas in the belief that innovation is the way to get ahead. In other organizations, people emphasize quantitative analysis in the belief that controlling risk is the way to get ahead. These generally held beliefs are rarely based on a clear statement of values; more often, they are based on observation of the career paths taken by others over the years and recognition of common patterns that tend to characterize successful and unsuccessful executives.

Myths are the stories or legends that persist about an organization and its leaders, reinforcing the core values or beliefs. For example, in one corporation, the myths surround "close calls" in making travel connections; they symbolize the emphasis on spending the most possible time with customers and minimizing time wasted in transit. Such stories are not pieces of trivial information— they are part of a body of clues or signals that transmit the culture to new members of the organization and reinforce that culture for existing members.

Traditions are repetitive significant events in an organization, including such rituals as welcoming luncheons, promotion celebrations, special awards, retirement parties, and twenty-fifth anniversary dinners. These events inject a predictability into the organizational environment and are a basic means of perpetuating cultural values, whether they honor tenure, advancement, or a special accomplishment that is held in high esteem by the organization.

Norms are the informal rules that exist in organizations regarding dress, work habits, work hours, and implicit codes of interpersonal behavior. For example, in one corporation, the senior executives answer their own telephones; in another, all phone calls are screened by secretaries. The first corporation is known for its open-door policy and for the openness of communications among levels of management. In a third corporation, it is expected that all business travel should be done either before or after business hours; this rule of conduct is not written down in any employee handbook or policy guide, but it is generally accepted as representing "the way things are done around here."

Such values, beliefs, myths, traditions, and norms are the elements that define an organization's culture. They are difficult—almost impossible—to measure and are often hard for people to articulate, but they are real and have to be managed as part of the process of implementing strategy.

The problem is that corporate culture is too big to be managed in the normal sense. There are too many variables, too many things to pay attention to. As one manager at the Colgate-Palmolive Company expressed it: "It's like punching a pillow. . . . You exert a lot of energy, but the results are so transitory. Nothing seems to really change, and you never know what to do next." The behavioral consequences of corporate culture are more tangible and observable than the culture itself. As a result, executives who are trying to change the strategy of an organization—and know that they need to change the behavior of managers—will be frustrated and discouraged if they focus too much attention on modifying or creating new values, beliefs, norms, and so on. What is required is a more manageable task—but one that still affects the cultural variables.

The Concept of Organizational Climate

In contrast to culture, which is the broadest and least tangible organizational influence on managerial behavior, the concept of organizational climate offers a more clearly definable and measurable vehicle for assessing and changing behavior in the workplace. Climate is more manageable than culture. Therefore, the best way to change corporate culture is to measure and manage organizational climate.

Climate is the label we use to describe six dimensions of the work environment that can be measured with relative precision. Extensive research based on the work of George H. Litwin and Robert Stringer (1968) at the Harvard Business School has shown that the six dimensions that comprise organizational climate have a direct and measurable impact on the motivation and performance of the employees of an organization. It is difficult to assess motivation or

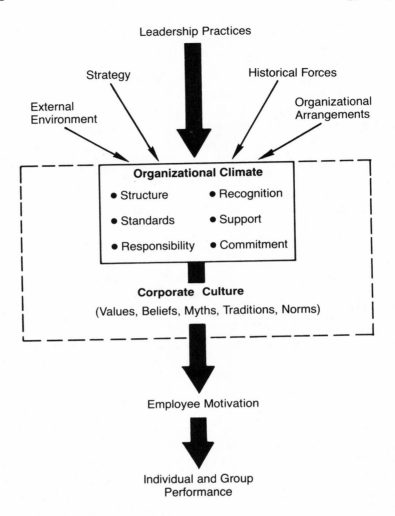

Figure 8–1. *An Organizational Performance Model*

to measure it, but it is possible to measure and manage climate. Figure 8–1 illustrates a simple model of organizational performance and shows how the concept of climate fits. We think of climate as a small part of the overall corporate culture. But because we have studied it so well and have learned how to manipulate it, climate is an ideal starting point for managing corporate culture.

Research has identified the following dimensions of organizational climate as important determinants of employee motivation and performance:

1. *Structure* reflects employees' sense of being well organized and of having a clear definition of their roles and responsibilities. Structure is high when people feel that everyone's job is well defined. It is low when there is confusion about who does what tasks and who has decision-making authority.

2. *Standards* measure the feeling of pressure to improve performance and the degree of pride employees have in doing a good job. High standards mean that people are always looking for ways to improve performance. Low standards reflect lower expectations for performance.

3. *Responsibility* reflects employees' feelings of "being their own boss" and not having to double-check decisions with others. A sense of high responsibility signifies that employees feel encouraged to solve problems on their own. Low responsibility indicates that risk taking and testing of new approaches tend to be discouraged.

4. *Recognition* indicates employees' feelings of being rewarded for a job well done. This is a measure of the emphasis placed on reward versus criticism and punishment. High-recognition climates are characterized by an appropriate balance of reward and criticism. Low recognition means that good work is inconsistently rewarded.

5. *Support* reflects the feeling of trust and mutual support that prevails within a work group. Support is high when employees feel that they are part of a well-functioning team and

when they sense that they can get help (especially from the boss) if they need it. Support is low when employees feel isolated and alone.

6. *Commitment* reflects employees' sense of pride in belonging to the organization and their degree of commitment to the organization's goals. Strong feelings of commitment are associated with high levels of personal loyalty. Lower levels of commitment mean that employees feel apathetic toward the organization and its goals.

We have developed a questionnaire that measures the relative strength of each of these climate dimensions (see table 8–1). The questionnaire can be completed in less than 15 minutes. Administration of this kind of climate survey is usually supervised by an outside consultant. This serves to protect the confidentiality of responses and makes the entire process more objective. Each manager who is participating in the survey gives a questionnaire to his or her subordinates. The subordinates complete the survey and mail the completed questionnaire in a sealed envelope to the consulting firm. All completed questionnaires are then processed by computer, and a report is generated that allows a company to size up its climate quickly, senior managers begin the process of managing corporate culture.

What Determines Organizational Culture and Climate?

A variety of factors determine the culture and climate of an organization. Research into these determinants is continuing, but the primary factors that drive culture and climate are those shown in figure 8–1.

Leadership Practices
Most studies have shown that the single most important determinant of an organization's culture and climate is the day-to-day behavior of the boss. The leader of a work group has a powerful influence on the expectations of its members. Often, the quickest way

Table 8–1
Climate Questionnaire Items

Climate Dimensions	Questionnaire Items
Structure: The sense employees have of being well organized; of having a clear definition of their roles and responsibilities.	The jobs in this Organization are clearly defined and logically structured. In this Organization it is sometimes unclear who has the formal authority to make a decision. In some of the projects I've been on, I haven't been sure exactly who my boss was. Our productivity sometimes suffers from lack of organization and planning.
Standards: The feeling of pressure to improve performance and the degree of pride employees take in doing a good job.	In this Organization we set very high standards for performance. In this Organization people don't seem to take much pride in their performance. Around here there is a feeling of pressure to continually improve our personal and group performance. Our management believes that no job is so well done that it couldn't be done better.
Responsibility: The feeling employees have of "being their own boss"; of not having to double-check all their decisions.	We don't rely too heavily on individual judgment in this Organization; almost everything is double-checked. Around here management resents your checking everything with them; if you think you've got the right approach you just go ahead. You won't get ahead in this Organization unless you stick your neck out and try things on your own. Our philosophy emphasizes that people should solve their problems by themselves.
Recognition: The feeling of being rewarded for a job well done; the emphasis placed on reward versus criticism and punishment.	In this Organization the rewards and encouragements you get usually outweigh the threats and the criticism. There is not enough reward and recognition in this Organization for doing good work. We have a promotion system here that helps the best person rise to the top. In this Organization people are rewarded in proportion to the excellence of their job performance.
Support: The feeling of trust and mutual support that prevails in this organization.	You don't get much sympathy in this Organization if you make a mistake. When I am on a difficult assignment I can usually count on getting assistance from my boss and co-workers.

(Table 8–1 continued)

Climate Dimensions	Questionnaire Items
Support *(continued)*	People in this Organization don't really trust each other enough. I feel that I am a member of a well-functioning team.
Commitment: The sense of pride employees have in belonging to the organization; the degree of commitment to the organization's goals.	Generally, people are highly committed to the goals of this Organization. People here feel proud of belonging to this Organization. People don't really care what happens to this Organization. As far as I can see, there isn't much personal loyalty to the Organization.

Adapted from *Motivation and Organizational Climate*, George H. Litwin and Robert A. Stringer (Cambridge, Mass.: Harvard University Press, 1968), pp. 67, 200–207.

to change the culture and climate of the organization is to change the way the managers are managing. To the extent that a hierarchical chain of managers can synchronize their practices, climate change can be accelerated, because the climate of every work group is somewhat influenced by the leadership practices of the boss's boss, and so on. However, it is possible for an individual manager to modify his or her own work unit's organizational climate even if that manager's boss makes no changes.

Organizational Arrangements
The second most powerful determinant of culture and climate is what we call organizational arrangements—the formal organizational structure (including the design of tasks and jobs), the reward systems, the policies and procedures, the physical location of the organization, and the selection and staffing process. It is clear that these factors influence the tone of the workplace and that they create strong barriers or incentives to employee behavior. Formal organizational arrangements often determine the flow of information as well as perceptions of opportunities for advancement—and all of these affect culture and climate.

External Environment

The external environment in which an organization competes often plays an important role in determining the organization's culture and climate. Factors such as government regulation, economic conditions, competitive industry forces, and technology create pressure on organizations and their managers. All of these external forces have profound effect on the values and beliefs that develop within an organization. These forces manifest themselves in measurably different culture and climate profiles. For example, the culture and climate that characterizes a team of engineers working in a fiercely competitive high-technology industry will be markedly different from the culture and climate of a similar team of engineers working in a conservative, semimonopolistic public utility where technology is not changing.

Strategy

When it is properly communicated, an organization's overall strategy can have a profound impact on its culture and climate and, over time, can influence the development of values and beliefs in the organization. If a corporation has chosen an aggressive, growth-oriented strategy, for example, and has successfully aligned its goals, priorities, and resource allocations with this strategy, the organizational culture and climate will, over time, begin to reflect the strategic priorities (in this case, the climate dimensions of standards and responsibility would rise). Unfortunately, there is no guarantee that this will take place, which is why we recommend that explicit attention be paid to matching strategy and culture. The absence of a clearly articulated strategy also has implications for the organization's culture and climate. Often, low levels of structure and commitment are the measurable indicators of unclear strategic guidance from top management.

Historical Forces

An organization's history has a strong impact on the culture that develops over time and on the organization's climate profile. The circumstances surrounding the founding of the organization, the manner in which crises have been faced and resolved, and the organization's role models all can affect its culture and climate. For example, if an organization was founded by highly innovative engineers to provide leading-edge technology to the marketplace, these circumstances of the organization's birth may continue to influence the cultural values of the organization, probably resulting in a climate characterized by a high level of responsibility.

Managing Corporate Culture and Organizational Climate

The determinants of culture and climate provide executives with points of leverage in managing the organization's work environment. Because it is the most important determinant, the most important lever is the personal leadership demonstrated by senior managers. Our research and experience tells us that changing leadership practices is the best way to affect the climate and thus change the corporate culture. Three factors will determine the success of such change efforts:

1. How well the executive *plans* his or her culture management initiative: Is it clear what must change to support the new strategy? Do managers know how their leadership practices are perceived by employees? Can they focus on those aspects of leadership that have the strongest impact on the culture?

2. How well the executive identifies and deals with the *other determinants* of culture, particularly organizational arrangements: Are the formal reward, planning, personnel, and management information systems adjusted to fit the desired change in leadership practices? Are structural changes to be made?

3. How well the executive is able to *execute* the culture improvement plans: Does he or she have the experience, skills, and resources necessary to carry out the plan? Is a feedback mechanism in place to measure progress and help the executive make midcourse corrections?

A Step-by-Step Approach

We have developed the following step-by-step approach to culture management. Our approach stresses the fundamental causal relationships between leadership practices and organizational climate and corporate culture. Although the steps are sequenced according to our own successful experiences, we are aware of situations in which several steps can be combined, reordered, or even repeated. None should be skipped.

Step 1: Size Up the Current Situation

This sizing up should include a business review and a survey of the organizational climate. Harbridge House, The Forum Corporation, Delta Consulting Group, Hay Associates, and others have developed climate surveys that can be used for this purpose. (We prefer the questionnaire outlined in table 8–1.) The survey should be supplemented with interviews to capture anecdotal data about the current work environment and leadership practices.

Step 2: Establish Culture and Leadership Goals

Senior managers must determine the kind of work environment and leadership that is required by the new strategy and the new business circumstances. If our climate model is being used, executives can define what the climate profile should be by discussing the importance of each of the six dimensions. This helps make the culture and leadership goals more tangible, and achieving the goals thus becomes more manageable.

Step 3: Identify Climate Improvement Priorities

By comparing the current sizing up to the desired goals, executives will be able to identify gaps or areas that need to be modified. Once again, if our six-dimensional climate system is used, these areas can be more precisely defined. All members of the management team then share a common vocabulary, which makes it easier to describe the problems and opportunities and allows more time to be spent on the next three steps.

Table 8–2
Leadership Practices That Affect Organizational Climate

Climate Dimensions	Practices
Structure: The sense employees have of being well organized; of having a clear definition of their roles and responsibilities.	Establishing clear, specific performance goals for your subordinates' jobs. Clarifying who is responsible for what within the group. Making sure tasks and projects are clearly and thoroughly explained and understood when they are assigned.
Standards: The feeling of pressure to improve performance and the degree of pride employees take in doing a good job.	Setting challenging performance goals and standards for your subordinates. Demonstrating personal commitment to achieving goals. Giving your subordinates feedback on how they are doing on their jobs.
Responsibility: The feeling employees have of "being their own boss"; of not having to double-check all their decisions.	Encouraging your subordinates to initiate tasks or projects they think are important. Expecting your subordinates to find and correct their own errors, rather than doing this for them. Encouraging innovation and calculated risk taking in others.
Recognition: The feeling of being rewarded for a job well done; the emphasis placed on reward versus criticism and punishment.	Recognizing subordinates for good performance more often than criticizing them for poor performance. Utilizing recognition, praise, and other similar methods to reward subordinates for excellent performance. Relating the total reward system (compensation, recognition, promotion) to the excellence of job performance rather than to other factors such as seniority, personal relationships, etc.
Support: The feeling of trust and mutual support that prevails in this organization.	Setting challenging performance goals and standards for your subordinates. Demonstrating personal commitment to achieving goals. Giving your subordinates feedback on how they are doing on their jobs.
Commitment: The sense of pride employees have in belonging to the organization; the degree of commitment to the organization's goals.	Communicating excitement and enthusiasm about the work. Involving people in setting goals. Encouraging subordinates to participate in making important decisions.

Step 4: Identify Key Leadership Practices

Once climate improvement priorities have been set, the critical aspects of leadership can be identified. Our climate research has shown that certain leadership practices have a powerful impact on each of the six dimensions of climate. These relationships are presented in table 8–2. It is important at this stage to be brutally frank and to specify *which* executives need to modify their leadership behavior and *how* the behavior should change. Having a checklist such as that provided by our list of practices in table 8–2 allows us to be quite specific at this phase. Steps 1–3 can be accomplished without the help of consultants; Step 4 can't. Consultants are best suited to help senior executives "look in the mirror" and critique their own management styles. Without the assistance of an outside third party, it is unlikely that Step 4 will be successful.

Step 5: Analyze Systems That Support Leadership

The formal (and sometimes informal) systems of the organization must be examined to ensure that they support the leadership practices executives wish to emphasize. The following are the most important things to examine:

How goals are set.

What goals are set.

What results are measured.

How rewards are distributed.

How performance is evaluated.

What (and when) information is communicated (and to whom).

How career decisions are made.

Step 6: Develop a Climate Management Plan

Any broad-scale initiative requires a written action plan, and culture management is no exception. The climate management plan should include specific actions, timetables, and accountabilities. Commitments should be made to measure and monitor the climate in 9 to 12 months to see whether the culture is moving in the desired direction.

Step 7: Publicize Culture Management Initiatives

No matter how comprehensive or how skimpy the climate management plans turn out, *all* efforts to change the corporate culture should be widely publicized. Culture management should become a topic for discussion at all levels of the organization. Managers should know that they are expected to act in new ways. They need to be constantly reminded of the themes of the new culture. Role models should be praised publicly. This kind of publicity will help legitimize the new culture management initiatives and will help solidify and reinforce the changes as they occur.

Summary

Explicit efforts by executives to manage organizational culture and climate often determine the success of new business strategies. The organizational climate concept provides a useful starting point for changing the culture of an organization. Research clearly indicates that managers are the driving force behind the culture and climate of organizations. Therefore, managers must be the target of culture change efforts. Senior executives have the opportunity and the responsibility to direct the culture of their organization so that it motivates the intended performance from employees. When they do so, the individuals within the organization—and the organization itself—can achieve the levels of productivity and performance necessary to achieve business strategies and goals.

9

How to Implement Strategic Change

Managing change is now recognized as one of the critical responsibilities of senior executives—and few changes can be as disruptive and as difficult to manage as a change in business strategy. Even the most experienced managers fall into the strategy traps outlined in this book. In previous chapters we have offered specific advice about how to avoid or how work your way out of each of the traps. In this chapter, we describe a series of basic rules and techniques for managing change that should be applied to your efforts to implement strategy.

Dr. David Nadler and his colleagues at Delta Consulting Group, a New York-based consulting firm, have developed a general framework for managing complex organizational changes. They have identified three problem areas that must be addressed:

1. *The political system:* The political dynamics of the organization must be shaped to support the proposed change.

Adapted with permission from material copyrighted by Delta Consulting Group, Inc., New York, NY. For further details, see David A. Nadler, "Managing Organizational Change: An Integrative Perspective," *Journal of Applied Behavioral Science* 17(2), 1981; D.A. Nadler and M.L. Tushman, "A Congruence Model for Diagnosing Organizational Behavior," in D.A. Nadler, M.L. Tushman, and N.G. Hatvany (Eds.), *Approaches to Managing Organizational Behavior: Models, Readings, and Cases* (Boston: Little, Brown, 1981); Delta Consulting Group, *Concepts for the Management of Organizational Change* (New York, Delta Consulting Group, 1980).

2. *Individual motivation:* People need to be sold on the change; resistance must be managed so that people will react constructively to the proposed change.

3. *Managing the transition:* During the implementation period, effective control mechanisms must be put in place to ensure a smooth transition from the old to the new.

Each of these problem areas must be managed when implementing a new strategy. People tend to play politics, and many individuals want to hang on to the old strategy and resist the new; thus, there is a real threat of losing control during the early implementation phases (when it sometimes seems as if there is *no* strategy).

Nadler has developed a list of twelve techniques for dealing with these problems (see table 9–1). We believe these techniques can be readily applied to help managers avoid our strategy traps—especially the implementation traps. Our experience with this framework has been very positive. Working with Delta Consulting Group, we have helped such companies as Citibank, Xerox, AT&T, PepsiCo, and Colgate-Palmolive in managing their way through complicated organizational changes.

Shaping the Political Dynamics

Nadler has suggested four guidelines for shaping the political dynamics in an organization so that change will be more easily accepted. All of these guidelines are important for managing strategic change.

1. Get the Support of Key Power Groups
To build a critical mass for change, key players have to be identified and won over. Senior managers must analyze the power structure of the organization to identify who the key players are. One useful technique for doing this is to divide managers and employees into three categories: those who must *make* the change happen (their support is critical), those who must *help* it happen (their support is

Table 9–1
Techniques for the Management of Organizational Change

Shaping the political dynamics
1. Get the support of key power groups
2. Demonstrate leadership support of the change
3. Use symbols
4. Build in stability

Motivating constructive behavior
5. Create dissatisfaction with the current state
6. Obtain appropriate levels of participation in planning/implementing change
7. Reward desired behavior in the transition to the future state
8. Provide time and opportunity to disengage from the current state

Managing the transition
9. Develop and communicate a clear image of the future state
10. Use multiple and consistent leverage points
11. Use transition devices
12. Obtain feedback about the transition state; evaluate success

less critical); and those who need only *let* it happen. By concentrating on the "make it happen" group, one can more effectively and efficiently shape the political dynamics.

Efforts to build support necessarily include a wide range of power-politics techniques. Allowing important people to participate or otherwise "own" the change often works wonders. Sometimes, it is necessary to strike deals or bargains. Sometimes, the only way to avoid a political barrier is to isolate the individual or group who is against the change. As a last resort, it may be necessary to remove the obstacle (by transfer or termination).

As suggested in chapter 4, getting the support of key power groups is a crucial step for smooth implementation of a new business strategy. If the strategic planning process is participative, the planning workshops will be the forum for identifying key players and determining who is for and who is against the new strategic plans.

2. Demonstrate Leadership Support of the Change
Certain kinds of leadership seem to work best in managing the political dynamics of change. *Visible* leadership is important; *articulate* leadership is important; and *proactive* leadership is important. Whenever there is a major change, a certain power vacuum is created in the organization. Visible, articulate, and proactive leaders can fill this vacuum and create momentum for change by acting as role models and confidence builders for other managers and employees.

As discussed in chapter 6, strategy implementation requires this kind of leadership support. Enthusiasm for the new strategic direction depends on the amount of confidence the senior executives can instill in the organization. Members of the planning department or other staff departments should not be used as the only spokespeople for a new strategy. Top executives must be seen and heard to build the necessary momentum for change.

3. Use Symbols
Symbols—such as slogans, pictures, and the like—help people identify with the future order and create the impression of broad-scale support for change. Symbolic acts (such as a promotion, moving an office, or a termination) can be important signals of change and can shape political dynamics. Often, the most effectively implemented strategies are supported by easily remembered phrases or other symbols. If a new customer group is to be targeted, for example, it may be represented symbolically by a person. Sanger-Harris, a Dallas department store, actually named its "typical" upscale female customer Sally Harris.

4. Build In Stability
Nadler has emphasized the importance of minimizing excess anxiety by providing anchors for people during a large-scale change. These anchors create a sense of stability. During periods of great change, employees often assume that *everything* is changing, so it is important to stress what *isn't* going to change. This reduces unwarranted fear and prevents the rumor mill from getting out of hand.

The most effective tool for building in stability during the implementation of a new business strategy is the implementation plan itself. This plan should articulate what will and what won't be changing. As noted in chapter 6, it is very difficult to slow down strategic change once the new strategy has gained momentum. Rather than trying to build in stability along the way, it is best to build it in up front and make the anchors very clear in the implementation plan.

Motivating Constructive Behavior

Nadler has also suggested four guidelines for dealing with the issue of motivating constructive behavior. Each of these guidelines offers senior managers an opportunity to manage the implementation of strategic change more systematically.

5. Create Dissatisfaction with the Current State

If people believe that the current state is wonderful, it is not hard to understand why they would resist change. Thus, managing change involves "unfreezing" people from the present so that they'll more readily embrace the future. A variety of techniques can be used to do this. Frightening people into changing often works well. For example, if employees believe that not changing will cost them their jobs, they will be more motivated to change. The best way to create dissatisfaction with the current state, however, is to generate information that supports the need for change. The more actively managers and employees participate in the gathering of this information, the more they will believe it and the more they will understand its consequences.

Implementing strategic change requires that this technique be broadly applied. The best opportunity for creating dissatisfaction with the current state is during the strategy formulation process. As suggested in chapters 7 and 8, the process should include a careful sizing up of the current state of affairs. If the current state is unsatisfactory, the entire management team will soon reach this conclusion and thus be more motivated to adopt a new strategy for the future.

6. *Obtain Appropriate Levels of Participation in Planning/Implementing Change*

No action area is more important for motivating change than this one. High levels of participation create excitement, ownership, and commitment. But participation takes time, creates conflict, and sometimes causes confusion. The issue is to decide where, how, and when to use participation.

Opportunities for effective participation are greater during the early stages of a change. Participation in planning is more important than participation in implementing. (Like it or not, everyone is usually forced to participate in implementing a major organizational change, so there is not likely to be an increase in ownership or commitment at that point.) Nadler has emphasized that there are many different ways to involve people in changes. People can be used as experts, as representatives, as members of task forces, or as sounding boards. All of these roles increase the levels of participation and help motivate people to join (rather than fight) the change. Our experience is that *how* participation is achieved is less important than the fact that it *is* achieved.

In this book, we have emphasized time and time again the importance of applying this technique in the formulation and implementation of business strategies. If it is done right, the participative planning process outlined in chapter 7 not only should help managers and employees let go of the old order but should also increase their overall levels of motivation, commitment, and enthusiasm for the new strategy. Following this technique will avoid the "what they don't know won't hurt them " trap and the "sloppy communication" trap.

7. *Reward Desired Behavior in the Transition to the Future State*

If people are expected to change, they must be rewarded for changing. Both formal and informal rewards need to be managed. Often, the formal systems (compensation, appraisal, promotions) lag behind organizational changes by a year or more. Senior managers must realize this and must provide informal rewards and recognition until the formal systems catch up.

Strategic change is usually very difficult to manage in this regard. By definition, the new strategy has few formal rewards tied to it. Therefore, the use of *informal* reward mechanisms is critical. As discussed at length in chapter 5, senior managers must move quickly to align their reward systems with new strategies.

8. Provide Time and Opportunity to Disengage from the Current State

People need time to let go. There is a natural attachment to the way things are, and managing change effectively means allowing people a chance to mourn the old order before embracing the new. Ceremonial events, such as dinners, closing day ceremonies, and farewell speeches, serve this purpose and often help people deal with their sense of loss. Although some senior executives may wish to implement a new strategy in a "businesslike" way, this technique suggests that a little "hoopla" can go a long way. We recommend, therefore, that new strategies be implemented with fanfare and ceremony. Not only will this galvanize the organization's energies around the new strategy, it will also allow people to say good-bye to the old strategy. It is important that executives make people feel *good* about the old strategy, however. If it is attacked too openly, feelings of guilt and anger can overwhelm commitment to the new strategy. The most appropriate message should be that the old strategy was good in its day, but now it's time to move on to a brighter future with a new set of priorities.

Managing the Transition

The final four guidelines in Nadler's framework help executives manage the transition from the old to the new. As with the first eight, we have found that these guidelines are directly applicable to managing strategic change.

9. Develop and Communicate a Clear Image of the Future State

Transition periods are always confusing, uncertain, and somewhat out of control. Employees often don't know what is expected of them. It is very hard to manage toward something when you don't know what that something is. For these reasons, executives must develop as clear and complete a *vision* of the future as possible. Even when the end result is unclear, senior managers should communicate a consistent and forceful image of the new order. This is the best way to reduce the inherent ambiguity of change.

It is especially important that a clear image and vision of the future be created during periods of strategic change. Vague, wishy-washy descriptions of the benefits, advantages, and characteristics of the future will not allow the organization to move ahead with confidence. The inevitable anxiety generated by a new business strategy can best be managed when tomorrow's leaders take charge today. Clarity is much more important than accuracy, and executives should not worry about the predictive validity of their statements. Rather, they should seek to create an exciting and meaningful vision of the future.

10. Use Multiple and Consistent Leverage Points

All major changes involve many aspects of the organization. Tasks, people, systems, structures, informal arrangements, and the culture or climate all must be aligned if the organization is going to work smoothly. Executives must understand the systemic nature of changes and must aggressively manage multiple aspects of the change.

The use of multiple leverage points was highlighted in chapter 6. No organization can successfully implement a new strategy without changing its mix of resources, people, organizational structure, and management systems. The more the new strategy varies from the old, the more important it will be to use multiple and consistent leverage points for implementing it.

11. Use Transition Devices

By definition, the *transition* from an old order to a new order is different from either the old or the new. Special devices must be used to maintain control of the organization during this period. Nadler has suggested several tools that can be used:

A transition manager can be appointed.

A separate transition budget can be created.

A transition task force can be identified.

A transition plan can be drawn up.

Transition structures (such as dual management systems) can be established.

The most effective device for managing the transition during periods of strategic change is the strategic planning committee or task force. If properly constructed, such task forces or committees can serve as mechanisms to increase control during the shift from the old strategy to the new. Once again, it is important to stress the need for a complete strategy implementation plan. As outlined in chapter 6, this plan should include enough detail to see the organization through the turbulent transition period.

12. Obtain Feedback About the Transition State; Evaluate Success

Normal feedback processes often breakdown during periods of great change. Unfortunately, this is the time when it is most important that executives keep in touch with their organization. Therefore, it is critically important that they create new channels to obtain feedback. Formal methods (such as interviews and focus-groups or customer surveys) should be supplemented with informal methods (such as senior management meetings, breakfast meetings with various employee groups, field trips).

It is particularly important that such supplemental feedback mechanisms be used during the early stages of strategic change. Particular attention should be focused on feedback from *customers*. Collecting market information is probably as important as collecting organizational information for managing strategic change.

Postscript

In 1984, *Business Week* measured the success of the business strategies of thirty-three randomly selected companies that were written up in the magazine in 1979 and 1980. They discovered that nineteen of the thirty-three strategies didn't work according to the plans laid out by the top executives of the companies studied. As *Business Week* commented, "19 failed, ran into trouble, or were abandoned, while only 14 could be deemed successful." Fourteen out of thirty-three is a pretty lousy hit-rate for strategies that have been formulated and articulated in sufficient detail to appear in print in *Business Week*. We would have guessed that these strategies were the cream of the crop—the ones most likely to succeed. But 58 percent of them flopped.

Obviously, strategies fail all the time. Although none of *Business Week*'s sample companies was described in this book, our experiences are probably mirrored in those thirty-three organizations. Falling into strategy traps is so common as to be unremarkable. The trick is to learn from past mistakes and try to avoid falling into the same trap twice.

We hope this book will help executives formulate and execute winning strategies. We've described practical models that can be used to guide strategic thinking and techniques that provide insight into effective strategy implementation. More concrete tools to help executives avoid strategy traps can be found in the sample workbooks presented in the appendixes. These workbooks are meant to be used by *teams* of managers as part of a participative approach to strategic planning. The importance of such a team approach to strategy cannot be overstated. As we have emphasized throughout this book, successful strategy implementation begins when the strategy is formulated. One of the biggest lessons we've learned about avoiding strategy traps is that the *content* of the strategy is often less important than the *process* used to develop it. We hope that this book has provided managers with ideas on how to manage *both* the content and the process more effectively.

Appendixes: Checklists for Improving Strategy

We have developed three workbooks in our consulting practice as tools for executives to use in formulating strategies. Each workbook presents a systematic approach to one aspect of the strategy formulation process. The first covers industry analysis, the starting point for strategic planning. The second covers competitor analysis, a frequently overlooked component of the strategy formulation process. The third covers the concept of competitive advantage—how to select a generic strategy and identify potential sources of long-term advantage. These workbooks were designed for particular clients; we've altered them for presentation here to make them applicable beyond the business and industry for which they were developed.

Appendix A: Industry Analysis Workbook

This workbook, which was prepared for several clients, provides a step-by-step approach to conducting an industry analysis. It is based on Michael Porter's (1980) *Competitive Strategy* text and allows executives to apply Porter's concepts to their industry. It requires that managers systematically analyze the power of buyers, suppliers, potential entrants, substitute products, and rivalry among firms. Industry analysis provides a means of making explicit the hidden assumptions about industry forces. Until the executive team has brought these assumptions to the surface, tested them, and come to agreement on them, it should not formulate strategies.

Appendix B: Competitor Analysis Workbook

This workbook, initially prepared for business managers of a financial service company, provides a guide for collecting and analyzing data on competitors. It can be used by account officers; field, regional, or zone sales managers; and business managers. The workbook has an action orientation and is designed as a means of identifying opportunities to open new accounts, expand the business geographically, and attack competitiors where they are weakest.

Appendix C: Competitive Advantage Workbook

This workbook, prepared for the executives of a major consumer goods company, provides a step-by-step approach to identifying sources of competitive advantage and formulating business strategies. It should be noted that, for this client, it was determined that an analysis of the external environment should include two groups of buyers: the trade and the final consumer of the company's product. As with the workbooks in Appendixes A and B, this workbook can be used in conjunction with the "how to" strategic planning model outlined in chapter 7.

Appendix A
Industry Analysis Workbook

Five competitive forces are present to some degree in all industries. These forces emanate from:

Buyers

Suppliers

Barriers to Entry

Substitute Products/Services

Competition/Rivalry among Firms

The collective power and balance of these forces largely determine the industry structure and, consequently, the viable strategic alternatives available to individual companies competing within that industry.

As an initial step in a thorough strategic analysis, it is critical to accurately assess the power exercised by each of these five forces. In analyzing your industry, the following exercises—one for each force—will provide you with a structure for this assessment. In each exercise, you are to answer all of the questions as thoroughly as possible. If you lack specific information, make the most reasonable assumptions you can.

Exercise 1: Buyer Power[a]

Buyers exercise power in an industry primarily through their ability to bargain—whether for lower prices (either with one firm or by playing several firms against each other as in competitive bidding), for higher quality, for more or better services, and so on. To the extent that buyers in general or a specific buyer group exercises a great deal of power, industry profitability is diminished. For example, the United States Air Force, as the sole or, on some occasions, the first buyer of a new fighter aircraft, is able to exert considerable power over the manufacturer in terms of both price and delivery.

Buyer power is a driving force in other industries as well. For example, in the word processing equipment industry a small business wishing to purchase a single stand-alone system possesses little or no real bargaining power while a large purchaser (e.g., a major bank) that orders several hundred systems is able to exercise its power and negotiate for quantity discounts, dedicated service teams, and the like.

---

[a]See Porter (1980), *Competitive Strategy,* pp. 24–27.

When assessing buyer power, it is often useful to speak in terms of buyer groups (i.e., organized clusters of individual buyers). In the word processing equipment industry example above, two buyer groups were referred to: small buyers—purchasers of single stand-alone systems, and large buyers—purchasers of several hundred systems. Generally buyer groups can be organized along several dimensions:

Size of purchase (e.g., large buyers, small buyers).

Frequency of purchase (e.g., one-time buyers, repeat buyers).

Industry (e.g., chemical industry buyers, automotive industry buyers).

Geographic location (e.g., far west buyers, northeast buyers).

Wealth, profitability, or liquidity.

Use of product (e.g., end user, distributor).

Although numerous buyer groups can be defined in any industry, not all of the groupings make sense in terms of assessing buyer power. Accordingly, the rule of thumb for developing relevant buyer groups is to select the dimension (e.g., size of purchase) or dimensions which for that group demonstrate the highest degree of variance in terms of exercisable power.

In the word processing equipment industry, for example, buyers grouped by size of purchase is a more useful segmentation than buyers grouped by geographic region. Clearly, little difference in power exists between buyers in the south and buyers in the northeast. Consequently, strategic approaches to buyers in both of these geographic regions should be similar. In contrast, major variations in exercisable power do exist between large buyers and small buyers regardless of their geographic locations. Accordingly, the strategic approaches to each of these buyers should reflect this difference. Grouping buyers by size of purchase rather than by geographic region provides a more useful market segmentation, correlating variations in power with size, something that is readily identifiable.

The following questions will help you analyze buyer power in your industry. Be sure to answer them completely.

A.   List the most meaningful groups of buyers in your industry and explain why they are "meaningful."

Buyer Groups	Why Meaningful

B.   For each buyer group listed above, answer the following questions. When your answer represents a source of power for the buyer group, indicate whether it is a "Significant" source of power (enter a "2" in the matrix); a "Moderate" source of power (enter a "1"); or "Not" a source of power (enter a "0"). After answering all of the questions, total the numbers for each buyer group.

	Buyer Groups				
1. Is the buyer group concentrated—i.e., comprised of a few dominant buyers? (If yes, a source of power.)					
2. Does the buyer group purchase large volumes relative to the seller's sales? (If yes, a source of power.)					
3. Do the products purchased by the buyer group represent a significant fraction of their costs? (If yes, buyer will be prone to bargain for price; thus, a source of power.)					
4. Are the products purchased by the buyer group standard and undifferentiated—i.e., commodity like? (If yes, buyer can find other sellers; thus, a source of power.)					
5. Would the buyer group face significant costs by switching from one seller to another? (If yes, buyer will be prone to stay with current seller; thus, not a source of power.)					

	Buyer Groups				
6. Does the buyer group earn relatively low profits? (If yes, buyer will be prone to bargain for price; thus, a source of power.)					
7. Do members of the buyer group pose a credible threat of backward integration—i.e., can they make what they currently buy? (If yes, a source of power.)					
8. Is the seller's product relatively important to the quality of the buyer's product? (If yes, buyer will be prone to bargain hard for quality but less so for price; thus, a source of power.)					
9. Does the buyer group possess a good deal of information about the seller's business—e.g., profit margins? (If yes, a source of power.)					
10. Does the buyer group have expertise in the purchasing function? (If yes, a source of power.)					
Total (maximum of 20 for each buyer)					

C.   Which buyer groups have the greatest market power in your industry? Why? (Consider the totals calculated in the matrix as well as individual elements of power.)

Most Powerful Buyer Groups	Why

D.   Which buyer groups have the least market power in your industry? Why? (Consider the totals calculated in the matrix as well as individual elements of power.)

Least Powerful Buyer Groups	Why

E.   What conclusions can you draw about buyer groups in your industry? Strategically, as a competitor in the industry, on which buyer groups should you focus your marketing efforts? Why? How does this focus differ from your current strategy?

Conclusions:

Focus of Marketing	Why

F. What actions could be taken to check buyer power (e.g., forward integration)? Toward what results?

Actions to Check Buyer Power	Result

Exercise 2: Supplier Power[b]

Suppliers exercise power in an industry in a number of ways—by raising prices, by lowering the quality of purchased goods, by tightening payment and service terms, and the like. To the extent that suppliers in general or a specific supplier group exercises a great deal of power, industry costs increase and profitability diminishes. A recent and painful example has illustrated the profound impact that a supplier group—OPEC—can have on an industry—petroleum refining—when it chooses to exercise power. As the dominant source of crude petroleum, OPEC has exerted substantial price-setting power over the refining industry during the last eight years, resulting in a quadrupling of the price of crude petroleum.

Suppliers in other industries, however, often have very little power to exercise. Can manufacturers, for example, have little power over one of their major buyers, the beer industry. In fact, beer companies have not only played off can manufacturers against one another, but they have also integrated backward to produce their own cans.

As both of these examples illustrate, industry profitability may be highly dependent on the extent to which suppliers possess and exercise power.

---

[b]See Porter (1980), *Competitive Strategy,* pp. 27–28.

The following questions will help you analyze supplier power in your industry. Be sure to answer them completely.

A.   List the most meaningful major suppliers (or supplier groups, if appropriate) in your industry and explain why they are "meaningful."

Supplier Groups	Why Meaningful

B. For each supplier group listed above, answer the following questions. When your answer represents a source of power for the supplier group, indicate whether it is a "Significant" source of power (enter a "2" in the matrix); a "Moderate" source of power (enter a "1"); or "Not" a source of power (enter a "0"). After answering all of the questions, total the numbers for each supplier group.

	Supplier Groups				
1. Is the supplier group concentrated— i.e., dominated by a few companies— or is it more concentrated than the industry it sells to? (The more concentrated the group, the greater the source of power.)					
2. Are there viable substitutes to the products provided by the supplier? (If yes, powerful suppliers can be checked with substitute products; thus, not a source of power.)					
3. Is the industry an important customer of the supplier? (If yes, supplier is less prone to exercise power; thus, not a source of power.)					
4. Is the supplier's product important to the buyer's business? (If yes, a source of power.)					
5. Are the supplier's products differentiated? (If yes, moving from one supplier to another may be difficult; thus, a source of power.)					

	Supplier Groups				
6. Would significant switching costs be involved in changing from one supplier to another? (If yes, a source of power.)					
7. Does the supplier pose a credible threat of forward integration—i.e., can it make what its customers buy? (If yes, a source of power.)					
Total (maximum of 14 for each supplier)					

C.   Which suppliers (or supplier groups) have the greatest market power in your industry? Why? (Consider the totals calculated in the matrix as well as individual elements of power.)

Most Powerful Suppliers	Why

D.   Which suppliers (or supplier groups) have the least market power in your industry? Why? (Consider the totals calculated in the matrix as well as individual elements of power.)

Least Powerful Suppliers	Why

E.   What conclusions can you draw about suppliers in your industry? Strategically, as a competitor in the industry, on which suppliers should you focus your purchasing efforts? Why? How does this focus differ from your current strategy?

Conclusions:

Focus of Purchasing	Why

F.   What actions could be taken to check supplier power (e.g., backward integration)? Toward what results?

Actions to Check Supplier Power	Result

Exercise 3:   Power of Barriers to Entry[c]

When evaluating competitive forces, it is often instructive to look beyond the current competition to firms that may enter the industry in the future. Potential entrants can range from individual entrepreneurs, as in the case of the fragmented restaurant industry, to major firms that buy into an industry (e.g., Philip Morris' entry into the beer industry through the purchase of Miller Brewing Company). Whatever the form of entry, new entrants frequently have a relatively large impact on the industry structure through:

> The added capacity they bring.

> Their desire for market share.

> Their pricing strategy.

> Their innovations and/or expertise in marketing, distribution, production, and so forth.

Consequently, it is critical to examine the ease of entry that firms have to an industry in order to be prepared for new entrants or to change the industry structure to make entry more difficult.

Not all industries are equally vulnerable to new entrants. If the barriers to entry are low (e.g., if little capital or expertise is required) and industry profitability is relatively high, new entrants can be expected. If, on the other hand, the barriers to entry are high, as in the automotive industry, and industry profitability is relatively low, few new entrants can be expected.

The following questions will help you analyze the extent to which barriers to entry exist in your industry. Be sure to answer them completely.

---

[c]See Porter (1980), *Competitive Strategy,* pp. 7–17.

A. Answer the following questions by placing an "X" in the matrix to indicate whether each factor leads to high entry barriers "To a Great Extent," "To a Moderate Extent," or "To Little or No Extent."

	To a Great Extent	To a Moderate Extent	To Little or No Extent
1. To what extent is your industry characterized by high economies of scale—i.e., unit costs decrease as production increases?			
2. To what extent are firms in the industry highly differentiated—i.e., brand identification and customer loyalty exist for specific distributors (e.g., through services offered)?			
3. To what extent are the capital requirements for entry into the industry high?			
4. To what extent are switching costs high (i.e., do buyers pay a "fine" for switching to a new entrant)?			
5. To what extent are distribution channels limited or already captured by incumbent firms?			
6. To what extent do incumbent firms having favorable geographic locations with respect to buyers preclude new entrants from obtaining similar geographic advantages?			

	To a Great Extent	To a Moderate Extent	To Little or No Extent
7. To what extend do incumbent firms have proprietary knowledge, technology, and/or personnel that are not readily available to new entrants?			
8. To what extent does government policy limit or foreclose entry into the industry?			

B. What are the major barriers to entry in your industry? Why? (Consider your responses in the matrix.)

Major Entry Barriers	Why

C.   What specific steps can be taken to strengthen the entry barriers in your industry? (In answering this question, consider the entry barriers suggested in the matrix. Then determine whether actions could be taken to increase each of these barriers and project the results of such actions on the industry structure.)

Actions to Strengthen Entry Barriers	Result

Exercise 4:   Power of Substitute Products/Services[d]

All firms in an industry compete not only with each other but also with firms producing substitute products/services. In this context, substitute products/services exercise power primarily by imposing a limit on the price that can be charged for competitive products. Whenever that price exceeds a certain amount, buyers will tend to look for—and in some cases create—substitutes. In this manner, substitute products/services are able to limit both the profitability and growth of an industry.

Paint and wallpaper are examples of substitute products in the home decorating industry. They are generally interchangeable and both satisfy the same customer function,[e] home decoration. A number of other substitute products/services exist in other industries as well. In today's banking industry, for example, automatic tellers represent only one electronic funds transfer product substituting for the traditional check-writing mechanism. In this latter case, as with all product/service substitutes, the customer function is not changed—namely, the withdrawal or transfer of funds from one account to another—and is satisfied equally well through checks or the use of automatic tellers. For this reason, Deluxe Check Printers, the dominant company involved in the printing of checks, must look beyond its normal competition to companies like Digital and Burroughs in order to accurately assess the future of the check printing industry.

Substitute products/services that pose the greatest threat to an industry are those that:

Provide improved price performance relative to the industry's product(s).

Are produced by industries that earn high profits.

Are currently being marketed more aggressively than in the past.

The following questions will help you analyze the power of substitute products/services in your industry. Be sure to answer them completely.

---

[d]See Porter, *Competitive Strategy,* pp. 23–24.

[e]See Abell, *Defining the Business,* Chapter 8.

A.   In column 1, below, list the products/services of your industry. Then, for each product/service, record in column 2 the customer functions(s) it serves (e.g., refrigerators satisfy the customer function of keeping perishable foods at cool (safe) temperatures). Finally, in column 3 list any substitute products/services capable of satisfying the same customer function(s).

(1) Products/Services	(2) Customer Function(s)	(3) Substitute Products/Services

B.   Which of the above substitute products/services pose the greatest threat to—i.e., exercise the greatest power on—your industry?

C.   To what extent are particular buyer groups more attracted to substitute products/services than to your products? Why?

D.   What strategic conclusions can be drawn about substitute products/services in your industry? What implications do substitutes have for individual firms competing in the industry?

Conclusions:

Implications of Substitute Products/Services:

Exercise 5:   Power of Competition/Rivalry Among Firms[f]

Rivalry among competitors can be one of the most powerful forces in an industry. This rivalry, varying in intensity from one industry to another as well as among individual firms within an industry, largely determines how competitive battles are fought.

Avis and Hertz are a good example of two firms that compete fiercely in the automobile rental industry through advertising that focuses on service, price, and industry position. Because of their neck-and-neck competition, either company can expect strong retaliation from the other if it takes strategic actions—for example, by implementing unlimited mileage pricing, as was done recently by Hertz. Other examples of industries where the rivalry is intense are fast foods, where McDonald's and Burger King compete for choice locations, and computers, where IBM, Burroughs, Digital, and others compete in terms of product introductions, technological innovations, and the like.

The industries in which intense rivalry exists among competitors generally have certain characteristics, namely:

Competitors that are relatively equal in market strength.

Slow industry growth, causing firms to compete for market share in order to grow.

High fixed costs, leading firms to cut prices in periods of excess capacity.

Commodity-like products, allowing buyers to switch relatively easily.

Competitors that have different strategies/approaches to the market.

Competitors that either cannot afford to leave the industry (because of costly exit barriers) or do not want to.

An understanding of the nature and intensity of rivalry among firms in an industry is critical to a competitive analysis of that industry in that it provides valuable information on expected retaliatory moves.

The following questions will help you analyze the power of competition/rivalry among firms in your industry. Be sure to answer them completely.

---

[f]See Porter (1980), *Competitive Strategy,* pp. 17–23.

A.   Answer "Yes" or "No" to the following questions dealing with competition/rivalry in your industry by placing an "X" in the appropriate box.

	Yes	No
1. Is the number of firms in the industry high? (If yes, rivalry tends to be high.)		
2. Are the firms in the industry relatively balanced in terms of sales? (If yes, rivalry tends to be high.)		
3. Is growth in the industry relatively slow? (If yes, firms expand market share at each other's expense; thus, rivalry tends to be high.)		
4. Are fixed costs in the industry high? (If yes, firms tend to cut price in order to cover costs; thus, rivalry tends to be high. This frequently occurs in industries where capacity must be added in large increments—e.g., fertilizer plants.)		
5. Are storage costs in the industry high? (If yes, firms tend to sell off inventory cheaply during slow periods; thus, rivalry tends to be high.)		
6. Are costs associated with switching from one firm to another high for the buyer? (If yes, rivalry tends to be low.)		
7. Are products highly differentiated from one firm to another in the industry? (If yes, rivalry tends to be low.)		
8. Are competitors within the industry different in terms of strategies, personalities, and/or relationships with a parent company? (If yes, rivalry tends to be relatively high as competitors are not likely to understand each other, a necessary condition for market equilibrium.)		

	Yes	No
9. Do firms have high strategic stakes in the industry? For example, is it important for a diversified conglomerate to achieve success in your industry through a subsidiary, even if that subsidiary is unprofitable? (If yes, rivalry tends to be high.)		
10. Do high exit barriers exist in the industry? For example, are assets highly specialized or are costs encountered upon exit? (If yes, rivalry tends to be high.)		

B.   How much competition/rivalry exists in your industry? Why?

C.   What are the major sources of competition/rivalry in the industry? Why?

Sources of Competition/Rivalry	Why

D.   What actions, if taken by an individual firm in the industry, would stimulate retaliation from other firms?

Your Competitive Position

Given the current strategy of your business—whether explicit or implicit—and your industry analysis, summarize how you have positioned yourself vis-à-vis the five competitive forces.

Buyers	
Suppliers	
Barriers to Entry	
Substitute Products/Services	
Competition/ Rivalry Among Firms	

Appendix B
Competitor Analysis Workbook

Adapted with permission from material copyrighted by Harbridge House, Inc., Boston, MA.

Section I: Identifying Competitors

The first step in conducting a competitor analysis is identifying existing and potential competitors. The following questions will provide a guide to this end.

1. List the major companies competing in your market.

2. Group these competitors in segments (for example, national companies, regional companies, and so forth).

3. Identify the top three to four firms posing the greatest threat to you.

   • For your lead product:

• For your market:

Section II: Data Collection

It is important to collect a complete data package for each competitor you are going to analyze. For publicly traded companies, there is a variety of data sources available, as listed below. For privately owned firms or smaller subsidiaries of larger companies, the data collection task is frequently more challenging and may involve field research.

Data Source	Obtained	Used in Competitor Analysis
Annual reports for past three years.		
10K Reports.		
Program, product, and service brochures.		
Price manuals.		
Customer quotes and comments.		
Security analysts reports.		
Newspaper/magazine articles.		
Industry sources (D&B, S&P).		
"Rumors, word of mouth, heard on the street."		
Other.		

Section III: Competitor's History

The objective of this part of the competitor analysis is to determine *how* the competitor got to *where* and *what* it is today. The output of this exercise should include:

A short history of the competitor, indicating how the competitor became involved in the business, the development of the competitor's product lines/programs, financial performance, services, technological capabilities, geographic coverage, and innovations.

The lessons or trends based on the above.

Section IV: The Competitor Today

A.   Basic Data

1. Sales ($).

2. Profits ($) (%).

3. Number of offices and locations.

4. Capacity (access to capital).

5. Debt-to-equity ratio.

6. Number of employees, type of people in the field (order takers vs. consultants; passive vs. aggressive).

7. How field employees are organized.

8. Financials by product line (if available).

9. Products, services, programs, and quality of service.

10. Target markets.

11. Selling pitch.

12. Technology/process.

13. Pricing policies (collect actual price data over the past two years, by month if available, and compare the data to yours).

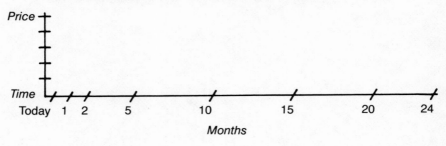

B. Conclusions from Basic Data

1. Is the competitor a price leader, a follower, or inconsistent? Explain.

2. What are the competitor's core products? Are we competing with these core products? How committed is the competitor to the product lines with which we compete?

3. What are the competitor's strengths?

4. What are the competitor's weaknesses/vulnerabilities?

C. Leadership

   1. Who runs the businesses we compete with in the competitor's
      organization?

   2. What are their backgrounds?

   3. What is their response time? Flexibility? Entrepreneurial flavor?

4. What are the parent company's influences on the competitor (centralized or decentralized decision-making)?

D. Competitor's Accounts and Markets

1. Which of the competitor's key accounts are vulnerable (if any)? Key account penetration (why).

2. Which of the competitor's other accounts are vulnerable (if any)? Account penetration (why).

3. What geograhic markets does the competitor serve? How well has each been penetrated?

4. What accounts has the competitor lost in the past two years? Why?

5. Has the competitor recently obtained accounts or greatly increased penetrated accounts? Why?

   • Strengths?

• Weaknesses?

E. Competitor's Commitments

1. Technology.

2. Key accounts.

3. Core products.

4. Geographic markets.

.

5. Organizational structure.

6. Based on the above, what are the competitor's key commitments? How innovative and willing to change is the competitor?

F. Competitor Strategies

1. What are the competitor's key financial goals?

2. What are the competitor's growth expectations?

3. What is the competitor's generic strategy (focus, overall cost leadership, differentiation)?

4. Does the competitor have a vision of the future? What is it? How committed is the competitor to this vision?

5. How capable is the competitor of achieving this vision?

G. The Competitor and Its Environment

1. Characterize the economic environment in which you and your competitor compete.

2. Specifically, how have you performed vs. the competitor? Where and why have we won/lost:

• Key accounts.

• Penetration of key accounts.

• Overall market share.

• Profitability.

• Growth (past and projected future).

• Geographic coverage in your area.

• Technology.

• Quantity and quality of people.

Section V: Competitor Response Profile

1. What offensive and defensive action is the competitor taking today?

2. What offensive and defensive action is the competitor capable of taking in response to changes in the environment?

3. What are the competitor's key response characteristics, strengths, and weaknesses? If the competitor takes action (see previous question), will the competitor be successful with it?

Section VI: Competitor Response to Our Strategy

1. What major actions have you recently taken in your market?

2. How has the competitor reacted to these actions?

3. Does the competitor view you as a major threat to its position? Explain its view of us.

4. What are the competitor's likely offensive or defensive reactions to these potential changes:

• Price increase.

• Price decrease.

• Product parameter changes.

- New product introductions.

- More aggressive selling.

- Going after one of the competitor's key accounts.

• Going after one of the competitor's non-key accounts.

Section VII: Conclusions, Recommendations, and Action Plans

1. What are our strengths and weaknesses vs. the competitor in our market?

2. What are the competitor's strengths and weaknesses vs. us in our market?

3. What opportunities do we have for offensive action?

4. What vulnerabilities do we have that require defensive reactions?

5. Actions that should be taken:

Actions We Control	Actions We Influence

The Action Plan	What It Will Accomplish	Resources Required	Who Will Do What	Time Frames

Appendix C
Competitive Advantage
Workbook

Introduction

The success or failure of our company depends on competitive strategy—establishing our competitive advantage so that we can either deliver our product at lower cost or offer unique benefits to the trade and consumer that justify a premium price. Competitive strategy defines how we will *win* in the marketplace.

Developing competitive strategies is the core of our planning process. We hope to build high-quality plans that will allow us to make better resource allocation decisions, better sales and market share projections, and provide us greater control over profits and return on investment.

This workbook will help you develop competitive strategies. The concepts and exercises are drawn from Michael E. Porter's framework (described in his books, *Competitive Strategy* and *Competitive Advantage*).

There are two types of competitive advantage a business may have or may develop over its rivals:

Cost Advantage.

Differentiation advantage.

A competitive cost advantage can lead to growth and profitability in several ways. A business with a cost advantage can lower prices to capture increased market share. It can take its cost savings and spend them on advertising, product enhancements, or additional services to increase market share. Or it can simply offer the same products/services at a price similar to that of competitors but capture a higher profit margin.

A business with a competitive differentiation advantage offers buyers greater value than competitors. Often, differentiation advantage stems from product features, service, brand name quality, or any of a number of attributes that are valued by certain buyers. Differentiation can lead to growth and profitability by allowing a business to capture a price premium or by capturing higher market share with a superior product/service offering.

Developing and maintaining competitive advantage(s) are key to the long-term success of any enterprise. If a business has neither a cost advantage nor a differentiation advantage, it will ultimately lose customers to competitors offering better prices or greater value.

This workbook will help you to develop a competitive strategy for your business. Specifically, this workbook will help you to:

Identify your business's competitive differentiation advantages and disadvantages with respect to both the trade and the consumer.

Identify your business's competitive cost advantages and disadvantages.

Identify alternative strategies to overcome competitive disadvantages and leverage competitive advantages.

Choose among alternative uses of available funds and other resources to maximize your sales and profitability.

Differentiation Advantages

A consumer goods company has two categories of buyers: trade and consumers. Within each category, there are many groups. For example, trade includes small independent grocery stores, multilocation supermarket chains, and everything in between. Consumers may be divided by demographics (women under 25, women 25 and older, men, etc.); by place of purchase (i.e., people who buy in supermarkets, people who buy from discount stores, etc.); or by any one of a number of other dimensions.

Each buyer group considers particular factors in choosing our product over competitive offerings. While attributes across buyer groups may be similar, groups typically weigh the importance of these factors differently. Supermarkets may place a high value on a manufacturer's price; a small grocery store may value liberal payment terms, others may value delivery, personal relations, or advertising and promotion support. Consumers usually value such factors as price, brand image, location/visibility on the shelf, or "what the kids want."

It is important to know what your buyers value as well as your ability to deliver those factors. Often one firm is better positioned than a competitor to deliver certain values. A business makes a product offering within the context of its existing organization, past practices, policies, manufacturing capabilities, image, and so on. These elements of a business are established over long period of time.

Bloomingdale's, for example, is better positioned than K Mart to deliver "style confidence" to buyers who value current styles. McDonald's services customers who value speed and standard quality; Fisher-Price services mothers who value sturdy/educational children's toys; Japanese auto manufacturers service customers who value high-quality compact cars; Levitz furniture stores, with its huge on-site warehouses, is better positioned to deliver many different furniture styles quickly.

Exercises I and II will help you to identify different buyer groups, the factors each group values (and why it makes buying decisions), and your business's ability to deliver those values relative to your key competitors.

Exercise I: Differentiation/Trade

1. In your business, what are the different types of retailers?

2. For each retailer group, identify and rank order what it values in choosing among us and our key competitors.

3. Are we better positioned or at a disadvantage relative to our biggest competitors in delivering what each retailer values? Why and how significant are the differences?

4. What would it take to further leverage our advantages, to develop an advantage, or to minimize a disadvantage? What would the payback be?

Retailer Buyer Groups	Critical Retailer Values

Competitive Advantage/Disadvantage	Possible Action(s)/Payback
Competitor A	
Competitor B	
Competitor C	

Exercise II: Differentiation/Consumer

1. In your business, what are the different types of consumers?

2. For each consumer group, what does it value in choosing among our brands and those of our competitors?

3. Are we better positioned or at a disadvantage relative to our competitors in delivering what each consumer group values? Why and how significant are the differences?

4. What would it take to further leverage our advantages, to develop an advantage, or to minimize a disadvantage? What would the payback be?

Consumer Buyer Groups	Critical Consumer Values

Competitive Advantage/Disadvantage	Possible Action(s)/Payback
Competitor A	
Competitor B	
Competitor C	

Cost Advantages

Cost is a critical source of competitive advantage or disadvantage, even in consumer goods industries dominated by "marketing mentalities."

For example, Heinz Ketchup's manufacturing operations have been configured to achieve the low-cost manufacturing position in the ketchup industry. Heinz successfully used this cost advantage in an aggressive price strategy to increase market share. Kellogg's has achieved several cost advantages over competitors and has directed much of the savings to advertising expenditures. Kellogg's now advertises at a level that competitors have difficulty matching.

Kimberly Clark realized that it could deliver an enhanced form-fitting diaper (Huggies disposable diapers) at a lower cost than that of Pampers, so it offered the form-fitting as a standard feature, which forced the manufacturer of Pampers to retool facilities and offer the form-fitting feature.

There are three steps involved in a sound analysis of competitive cost advantages:

Step One: Break the business into a chain of activities.

Step Two: For each activity identify the drivers of cost behavior.

Step Three: Analyze your position on cost drivers relative to key competitors.

Porter labels Step One as the identification of a business "value chain." Typically, a business has the following broad value chain of activities:

Inbound Logistics (e.g., raw materials)	Operations	Outbound Logistics (e.g., distribution)	Marketing & Sales	Service

Every business is different, however, and within each category in different businesses there are numerous subcategories of activities.

Step Two is the identification of cost drivers for each activity. Since each activity within a business's value chain may be influenced by different factors, separate activities must be analyzed to identify those factors that have the greatest impact on cost.

Typical cost drivers include:

Economies of scale (for some activities size means greater efficiency).

Shared cost with interrelated businesses.

Vertical integration.

Learning/experience (for some activities experience is what lowers costs the most).

Capacity utilization.

Facility locations.

Labor contract provisions.

Technology/equipment.

Step Three is determining where you stand relative to your key competitors. The exactness of these comparisons between your costs and those of a key competitor will depend upon the quality and quantity of the information available. While it is helpful to quantify cost differences, this is not always possible. Even without solid competitive cost accounting data, you can probably determine your approximate cost position on each business activity vis-à-vis a key competitor. The following is a hypothetical example:

1. Activity: Service of accounts.

2. Cost Driver: Capacity utilization and learning. As the number of accounts increases, our cost per servicing a single account decreases. Based on our experience, we estimate that a doubling of accounts yields a 20 percent decrease in cost per account.

3. Relative Position: We have one and one-half the number of accounts our competitor has. It costs us $25 per service call. Therefore, we have a cost advantage in this activity of approximately 15 percent (or amost $4).

Exercise III: Competitive Cost Advantage

1. Develop an activity chain for your business.

2. Identify the cost drivers within each activity.

3. For each activity, indicate if our costs are higher or lower than those of our key competitors. (Indicate how significant the difference is, estimating the numbers where possible.) State why you think the difference exists.

4. Identify what actions could be taken to develop or further leverage and advantage.

5. What actions could be taken to minimize disadvantages?

6. What resources would the proposed action(s) require? What would the payback be?

Activity	Cost Drivers	Competitive Advantage/ Disadvantage

Possible Action(s)	Resources Needed and Potential Paybacks

Exercise IV: Business Strategy Brainstorming

Introduction

Every business has limited resources with which to compete. In the previous exercises, you identified competitive cost advantages and disadvantages and potential differentiation advantages and disadvantages. It is also unlikely that your business has all the resources to act simultaneously on all of the issues identified. Therefore, the purpose of this exercise is to establish priorities and to think creatively about potential actions that will strengthen your business's competitive position.

Assignment

1. Review the output from Exercises I, II, and III, and identify the five major opportunities to develop a competitive advantage, leverage

an existing advantage, or overcome a significant disadvantage in your business.

2. For each major opportunity, identify alternative plans of action. Think of actions without regard to resources. Try to be creative— pretend that your business could do anything it wanted to do to "win."

3. For each plan of action, identify:
   a. Resources needed to execute the plan.
   b. Potential payback.

4. For each plan of action, identify additional information needs and research to be done prior to making a final decision. Indicate who will be responsible for this research, and set a deadline for completion.

Key Competitive Strategy Issue	Alternative Plans of Action

Resources Needed	Payback	Additional Research Needed/ Completion Date

Summary: Discuss and Choose Among Alternatives

Consider the following questions to guide your thinking in evaluating and selecting alternative strategies.

1. For developing a potential competitive advantage or further leveraging an existing competitive advantage:
   a. Will your plan lead to a clear cost or differentiation advantage relative to the competition?
   b. Will you be able to sustain the advantage or can competitors easily undermine it?
   c. Is your plan economically sound? Will the resource investment yield a good return?

2. For competitive disadvantages that you might consider minimizing:
   a. What would happen if you did nothing?
   b. Will the plan help you to overcome your disadvantage or help to achieve necessary cost or differentiation proximity to your competitor?
   c. Are there any opportunities to utilize your competitive advantage to overcome this disadvantage?
   d. Is your plan economically sound? Will the resource investment yield a good return?

Bibliography

Abell, Derek E. *Defining the Business*. Englewood Cliffs, N.J.: Prentice-Hall, 1980.

Drucker, Peter F. *Innovation and Entrepreneurship: Practice and Principles*. New York: Harper & Row, 1985.

Eccles, Robert G. *Transfer Pricing Problem*. Lexington, Mass.: Lexington Books, D.C. Heath, 1985.

Kotter, John P. *The General Managers*. New York: Free Press, 1982.

———. *Power and Influence*. New York: Free Press, 1985.

Levitt, Theodore. *The Marketing Imagination*. New York: Free Press, 1983.

Litwin, George H., and Stringer, R.A., Jr. *Motivation and Organizational Climate*. Cambridge, Mass.: Harvard University Press, 1968.

Mintzberg, Henry. *The Nature of Managerial Work*. New York: Harper & Row, 1973.

———. *Power In and Around Organizations*. Englewood Cliffs, N.J.: Prentice-Hall, 1983.

Nadler, David A. *Feedback and Organizational Development: Using Data-Based Methods*. Reading, Mass.: Addison-Wesley, 1977.

Nadler, David A.; Hackman, J.R.; and Lawler, Edward E. *Managing Organizational Behavior*. Boston: Little, Brown, 1979.

Peters, Thomas J., and Watterman, Robert H., Jr. *In Search of Excellence*. New York: Harper & Row, 1982.

Peters, Thomas J., and Austin, Nancy K. *A Passion for Excellence*. New York: Random House, 1985.

Pinchot, Gifford. *Intrapreneuring*. New York: Harper & Row, 1985.

Porter, Michael E. *Competitive Strategy*. New York: Free Press, 1980.

———. *Competitive Advantage*. New York: Free Press, 1985.

About the Authors

Robert A. Stringer, Jr. (M.B.A., Harvard Business School) is a management consultant specializing in strategy implementation and executive development. As senior vice president of Harbridge House, Inc. in Boston, Mass., he consulted with a wide range of companies, including PepsiCo., Xerox, Citicorp, Rexnord, Chemical Bank and Rockwell International. Mr. Stringer has served as a senior vice president of The Forum Corporation and was on the faculty of the Harvard Business School. He has written two other books: *Motivation and Organizational Climate* (with George H. Litwin) and *Men in Management* (with J.B. Kassarjian).

Joel L. Uchenick (M.B.A., McGill University) works with Mr. Stringer as a management consultant. As a principal with Harbridge House, Inc., Mr. Uchenick specialized in assisting clients formulate competitive strategies. Among the clients with which he has consulted are Citicorp; the New York Stock Exchange; Spear, Leeds & Kellogg; Chemical Bank; Filene's; Bank of Boston; W.R. Grace & Co.; McDonald's Corp.; Burroughs; Raytheon; DuPont; Phillips Petroleum; Merrill Lynch; Equitable Life; and Digital Equipment Corporation. Mr. Uchenick has written a book on real estate finance, *Condominiums* (with J. Dinkelspiel & H. Selesnick).